Berlitz®

Madeira

TOP 10 ATTRACTIONS

Madeira's hills and mountains. Venture out on spectacular scenic walks. See page 57.

The Adegas de São Francisco. Visit the oldest working wine lodge in Madeira. See page 29.

Monte. The fashionable hilltop town above Funchal is best known for its exhilarating toboggan rides. See page 41.

Jardim Botânico. Marvel at Madeira's extravagant flowers. See page 38.

Funchal's Museu de Arte Sacra. Outstanding Flemish paintings enjoy pride of place in this museum. See page 32.

Pico do Arieiro. Drive above the clouds to the top of Madeira's second-highest peak. See page 57.

Porto Santo. Relax on gorgeous golden sands on this nearby island. See page 66.

Madeira's lido complexes. Enjoy a dip. See page 89.

São Vicente. One of Madeira's most attractive villages, with volcanic caves nearby. See page 52.

Palheiro cottages. These traditional thatched cottages are still in use in the Santana region. See page 59.

A PERFECT TOUR

Day 1 — Funchal finery

Split your first day in the capital Funchal between the magnificent Quinta das Cruzes and the Adegas de Sao Francisco, the historic wine lodge. In the former you can check out the antiques and faded splendour of one of Funchal's grandest mansions, and in the latter you can taste Madeira's famous fortified wines.

Day 2 — Cable-car & market

Still in Funchal, take in the amazing views via cable car from Funchal's lush Jardim Botânico, and explore the gardens themselves on foot. Next, browse your way around the Mercado do Lavoradores, a busy, colourful spectacle, with leather goods, wickerwork, and handicrafts on sale alongside fruit, vegetables and fish.

Day 3 — Wicker toboggans

It's a short hop to the hilltop town of Monte, where you can explore the many local gardens, such as Jardim do Palácio do Monte, and indulge in a traditional downhill wicker toboggan ride, aided by drivers dressed in straw boaters.

Day 4 — Hill gardens

Spend the day exploring the Palheiro Gardens, most magnificent of Madeira's many splendid gardens. The hill-draped estate is a short bus ride from Funchal, and famous for its exotic plants, wild ravine, and gorgeous winter camellias.

OF MADEIRA

Day 6   Nuns' refuge

Next head to the equally spectacular Curral das Freiras, which you can reach via bus, car or organised tour, a 10km (6 miles) trip from Monte into another world. The village's name means 'Refuge of the Nuns', and it's encircled by a ring of mountains and was for a long time barely accessible to the outside world. It's an extraordinary sight, with the steep slopes around it dotted with terraces.

Day 8   Porto Santo

On the last day of your trip, fly or boat it over to the island of Porto Santo, with its 10km (6 miles) of golden beach. This tiny, mountainous, white-sand-fringed island is the ideal place to relax and spend the last day or so of your holiday.

Day 5   Pico do Ariero

You can take a bus tour to the summit of Madeira's third highest mountain, Pico do Ariero in the central highlands of the island. It's something of a moonscape, whose plunging barren volcanic landscapes glow russet red in the sunlight.

Day 7   São Vicente

The enchanting prettiness of Sao Vicente is worth the cross-island trip from Funchal. Not only will you see one of Madeira's most picturesque villages, but if you're feeling adventurous you can drive the heart-stopping, dazzling old coastal road from here to Porto Moniz.

CONTENTS

INTRODUCTION

A mere speck in the middle of the Atlantic Ocean, Madeira is a volcanic island thickly draped with vegetation, a colourful riot of flowers and fruit trees. Rugged mountains peek through the clouds, and microclimates hover over isolated villages. Spectacular cliffs crash down to the surf below.

Although the islands were known to Roman and Carthaginian sailors 2,000 years ago, Madeira was first settled only a few decades before Columbus made his way to America. It became part of the Portuguese empire after the great expedition teams of the 15th century claimed it for King João I. But Madeira is nearer to Africa than to Lisbon. It lies 600km (372 miles) off the coast of Morocco and nearly 1,000km (620 miles) southwest of the Portuguese capital.

Madeira is an archipelago, formed from volcanic eruptions many millions of years ago. The land is like an iceberg; massive mountains poke through the clouds, forming the mere tip of a submerged mass. Apart from Madeira itself, only one other island in the group is inhabited – the arid, much flatter holiday hideaway of Porto Santo. Christopher Columbus visited Porto Santo in the second half of the 15th century, and married the local governor's granddaughter.

Natural Wonders

Few places on earth can rival Madeira's wealth of natural gifts, especially in so small an area. The island is blanketed with flowers: birds of paradise display their bright orange, beak-like flowers in open fields. Fragrant hydrangeas line walking paths skirting the edges of mountain terraces. Private and public gardens burst with orchids, bougainvillea and jacaranda trees,

The terracotta rooftops of Funchal

Waterfalls dot the interior

while orchards and plantations heave with apples, pears, cherries, passion fruit, bananas and avocados.

In the mountains, water streams down from unseen springs: a one-hour walk might take you past half a dozen waterfalls. The cold waters around the island, once prime whaling territory, are now a marine sanctuary for whales, dolphins and seals. And all of this in year-round sub-tropical weather, with a southerly breeze and temperatures that average 22°C (72°F) in the summer and 17°C (63°F) during the winter.

Size and Population

Madeira seems much larger than its diminutive size, just 57km (35 miles) long and 22km (13 miles) wide. The terrain is so mountainous, and its roads so tortuous, that distances are magnified in terms of both time and effort. This can breed insularity; until fast roads were constructed in the decade since 1997, some villagers never travelled to the capital, Funchal, let alone to mainland Portugal. Yet young and upwardly mobile islanders do go off to seek their fortune, and the most successful return from overseas to build sumptuous villas.

But Madeira is not a simple Gauguin-like tropical paradise. With a history of emigration and return, of welcoming visiting merchants and, during a brief period of occupation, a garrison of British troops, islanders are a cosmopolitan mix. The populace is a stew of dark North African complexions and blonde, blue-eyed northern Europeans.

The Capital City

Funchal, the island's capital, major harbour and only city of any note, merely hints at Madeira's riches. The capital's white houses with tile roofs are clustered on picturesque hills sloping down to a steep bay, which makes for a pretty picture. The city is undeniably pleasant, but there are certain areas where the noise and traffic are just as bad as any other European city.

Desertas and Selvagens

As well as the two inhabited islands of Madeira and Porto Santo, the North Atlantic archipelago comprises another five uninhabited islands and numerous minor rocks and reefs. The islands fall into two groups: the Ilhas Desertas (Desert Islands) and the Ilhas Selvagens (Wild or Savage Islands).

The former consist of three islands, the nearest situated 12km (19 miles) southeast of Madeira. These desert islands are far from the Robinson Crusoe idyll: they are barren and inhospitable to the point where, aside from the occasional goat and rabbit, the most notable land creature is a large, poisonous black spider.

But the sea life around the islands is a different story. Dolphins and turtles are occasionally spotted, and there is a colony of very rare monk seals. Birdwatchers will relish the opportunity to see shearwaters and petrels. Marine biologists and nature conservationists are the only regular human visitors, for even though excursion boats frequently make trips to these isles in summer, landing is restricted to authorised persons only.

Meanwhile, the two Selvagens Islands, usually known as Grande (Large) and Pequena (Small), are Madeiran only in name. They lie 285km (177 miles) to the south and are actually closer to the Canary Islands than to Madeira. Like the Desertas, they are uninhabited and devoted entirely to nature conservation.

Almost half of Madeira's 270,000-strong population live in Funchal (pronounced 'foon-shawl'), where most of the island's tourism activity is centred. Here, visitors have a choice between the gleaming high-rise hotels of the *zona turista*, or the old-world hotels and distinguished *quintas* (rural estates) of Madeira's more peaceful past.

The Rural Interior

Funchal is less the sum of Madeira, though, than a gateway to the rest of the island, whose real charms begin in the hillsides just a few minutes outside the town. Spectacular gardens, including the Botanic Garden and Quinta do Palheiro, are only a short bus, taxi or cable car ride from the capital.

Small-scale agriculture dominates the island's landscape, and employs about a fifth of its people. Depending on the altitude, and whether you are on the warm south coast or

Funchal is a major harbour

the marginally cooler north coast, you will see terraces of bananas, and the vines that produce the grapes for fortified Madeira wine. There are windswept mountain peaks, craggy cliffs and emerald val-

Isolated villages

Some of the mountain villages of Madeira are so isolated that they did not begin to receive TV signals until the 1980s.

leys. From strategically situated lookout points (*miradouros*) you can take in these magical panoramas and look down on villages and terraced fields carved out of the mountains.

New roads and tunnels make driving around Madeira faster than before, though the best scenery is reserved for those who follow the hairpin bends of mountain roads and coastal lanes, getting sprayed by waterfalls and constantly stopping to enjoy spectacular vistas. Madeira is even better when explored on two feet. The island is heaven for anyone who enjoys being outside, whether your taste runs to gentle walks or hardcore hiking. Madeira's system of irrigation channels, known as *levadas*, carries water down from the mountains on gentle gradients and provides a ready-made system of trails. The canals–more than 2,100km (1,300 miles) of them wrap around the island–have level footpaths running along their entire length. Walkers of all ages and abilities need only find a *levada* to take in some of the finest countryside anywhere. Several of these walks, which are described later in this book (see page 86), are among the highlights of Madeira.

With such rapturous scenery and a climate that is consistently delightful, perhaps it would be unfair to expect nature to have bestowed miles of perfect sands on the island as well. Madeira has few beaches as such – although most coastal villages have swimming pools and sea access, and Calheta has an artificial beach. But if a chair by the pool just can't compare with waves lapping on sand, you will have to follow in the wake of Columbus and dock on the neighbouring island of Porto Santo, a popular day trip. The only other inhabited island in the archipelago, Porto Santo has a 9km (5.5 mile) beach running the length of its south coast, but few other attractions.

While some surely would find the notion of an island holiday with no beach time an unusual prospect indeed, perhaps it isn't such a tragedy that Madeira's shoreline crashes so violently into the ocean. Lack of sand has kept Madeira from becoming as popular as the Canary Islands or Mallorca. If Madeira had sandy beaches and cheap flights from Europe and North America, it would surely not have managed to preserve as much of its environment as it has. Yet tourism is eroding the island in other ways, as traditional farming gives way to a tourism economy, leaving the vertiginous hills untended and the picturesque terraces and *levadas* in decline.

Tourism and Madeira

For decades, Madeira has attracted a genteel, even anachronistic, form of island tourism. Afternoon tea and a jacket and tie at dinner are still de rigueur at the most elegant hotels. The typical visitor is still older and wealthier than in most holiday destinations, but times have changed – as they have across Portugal, which is no longer the forgotten backwater of Europe. Funchal's enlarged airport and increasing numbers of new hotels testify to local travel industry ambitions. Today Madeira is being discovered by younger travellers who might indulge in the spas and dining that world-class hotels offer, but are just as likely to seek out more modest accommodation up in the mountains and strap on their boots for serious hiking.

Madeirans, like most Portuguese, are a generally quiet and reserved people. Add to this geographical isolation and the difficulties for most of a harsh agricultural existence (where few have the machinery to help cultivate the tiny terraced fields) and you might well forgive the islanders if they seemed less than welcoming. Instead, you will find friendly people who, in spite of a 12-month season that for decades has deposited tourists from wealthier nations on their shores, are refreshingly hospitable. They are proud of the scenic beauty, delectable wines and exquisite hand embroidery for which their tiny island has rightly become famous.

Hoteliers, entrepreneurs and government officials may be eager to broaden Madeira's offerings and appeal, however, the allure of the island remains its absence of man-made attractions and its abundance of natural ones. Some people still suggest that Madeira is part of the lost continent of Atlantis, and, although it has become progressively easier to get there, the island still seems other-worldly.

Ponta de São Lourenço, Madeira's easternmost point

A BRIEF HISTORY

As befits a lush, tropical island stranded in the middle of the ocean, Madeira's origins are shrouded in fanciful legend. Some claim that the archipelago is all that remains of Plato's lost Atlantis, or that it is part of a landmass that once fused the continents of Europe and America. Recorded history begins in relatively recent times; in the early 15th century, just as the golden age of Portuguese discovery was erupting. Under the direction of Henry the Navigator, caravels set out from the westernmost point of the Algarve, in southern Portugal, in search of foreign lands, fame and wealth. João Gonçalves

The First Man on Madeira?

Some say that the first man to set foot on the island was not the Portuguese adventurer João Gonçalves Zarco but a 14th-century Englishman named Robert Machim (sometimes written Machin).

One version of the story is that Machim was a knight at the court of Edward III and sought to marry above his class, to a girl named Anne d'Arfet (or Anne of Hertford). The determined young lovers boarded a ship bound for France, which was thrown severely off course. The pair ended up shipwrecked on Madeira. Anne died of exposure soon afterwards, and Machim buried her by the bay where they had come ashore. Machim too died (it is said of a broken heart) and was buried alongside her by members of the same shipwrecked crew, who eventually escaped on a log raft and lived to recount the tragic tale.

Zarco, who is much more widely credited with the discovery of Madeira, was aware of the legend. He is said to have found the grave of the couple, naming the site Machico in honour of Machin. The couple's resting place is said to be beneath the Capela dos Milagres on the eastern side of Machico Bay (see page 63).

Zarco, sailing in the service of Prince Henry, made the first of many famous Portuguese discoveries: in 1418 he happened upon a small volcanic archipelago 1,000km (620 miles) from Lisbon.

Perhaps Zarco knew precisely where he was heading, having learned of the existence of Madeira from a Castilian source. After all, the waters of the Canary Islands, only 445km (275 miles) to the south, had supported busy shipping lanes for very

Henry the Navigator

nearly a century, and Genovese maps from the mid-14th century depict both Madeira and Porto Santo.

More likely, Zarco was heading for Guinea and storms forced him onto the beach of Porto Santo. If so, then he was fortunate, for he managed to land on the only large, sandy beach for hundreds of miles around.

Portugal's First Colony

The following year Zarco returned to claim the larger island he had seen from Porto Santo, and with him went Tristão Vaz Teixeira and Bartolomeu Perestrelo. They officially became the first men to set foot on the heavily forested island, naming it *Ilha da Madeira* – Island of Timber.

The Portuguese Crown, delighted with its first important discovery, embarked on a programme of colonisation. In 1425, King João I pronounced Madeira an official province of Portugal, and presented it as a gift to Prince Henry (Henrique). He, in turn, confirmed the land ownership rights to Zarco and

It seems certain that Madeira had never been inhabited before the Portuguese arrived in the 15th century. The first settlers found no Stone Age natives, as the Spanish had found in the Canary Islands, and no mysterious monuments to the past, as in the Balearics.

Teixeira, while Perestrelo was awarded Porto Santo.

Occupation of Madeira began in the early 1420s as a decidedly small-scale project: colonists arrived with only as much as they could carry from Portugal. They found plenty of water pouring down from the mountains, and more timber than anyone knew what to do with. So they set about clearing the land for agriculture, setting fire to massive tracts of forest. Legend says that a great fire burned for seven years on the island.

Energetic Agriculture

The fire provided the soil with a rich ash fertiliser, which complemented the luxuriant growing conditions of tropical sun and plentiful water. The Portuguese saw valuable economic opportunity in their new possession and sent for Malvasia grapes from Crete and sugar cane from Sicily in an effort to seed the island's first cash crops. The project was not a simple one. Colonists had to find enough level ground to grow crops on, and then solve the issue of irrigating them. Brute strength, without the aid of machinery, carved flat surfaces out of the mountains, and settlers built the terraces that are seen today on the steep slopes.

The problem of watering crops was solved by the irrigation system known as *levadas* – simply designed water channels that wound down from water sources on the verdant mountain tops. The *levadas* were largely built by slave labourers from Africa, whose primary employment was on sugar plantations. Madeirans traded sugar, the era's dominant luxury item, with Venice and Flanders, and proved skilful in the art of wine-making. The island's burgeoning economic significance propelled population growth, and by the middle of the 15th century Madeira was home to some 800 families. A census in 1514 recorded 5,000 inhabitants, not including slaves.

In 1478 Madeira welcomed a visitor who would greatly assist the island's future wine trade. Christopher Columbus, not yet a sailor of any renown, sailed to Madeira on an assignment to buy sugar cane. His sojourn was unsuccessful, as money failed to arrive for part of the shipment. Yet Columbus (Cristóvão Colombo in Portuguese) returned six years later, by which time evidence suggests that he had become an experienced sugar merchant. His later discovery of the New World brought prosperity to the Madeiran economy: the island's strategic location on the great East–West trading route meant that ships anchored and took on food, water and the valuable trading commodity of Madeira wine.

Columbus arrived as a sugar trader and became a resident

Columbus married Dona Filipa Moniz Perestrelo, the granddaughter of Porto Santo's first governor, and fathered a son on the island. Even today, there are those on Porto Santo who will tell you that it was during the time he spent there that Columbus learned

CRISTÓVÃO COLOMBO

navigation techniques, and found the inspiration to undertake his voyage of 1492.

Plundered by Pirates

From early in the 16th century, Madeira became the target of pirate attacks. Noticing the island's burgeoning wealth and repository of supplies, buccaneers from Morocco, Algeria and France invaded coastal settlements, plundered villages and left behind a trail of death and destruction. In 1566 Madeira suffered its worst disaster when the French pirate Bertrand de Montluc sailed into Funchal harbour with his 11-galleon armada and 1,300 men. He unleashed a 16-day reign of terror that left 300 Madeirans dead, stocks of sugar destroyed and the island plundered. By the time Lisbon mounted a rescue mission, the pirates had long fled.

As a result of the attack, Porto Santo, which had also been scourged by these villains of the seas, went on to build hilltop beacons to serve as early-warning systems, which allowed the citizens to defend themselves, or flee if necessary.

On the mainland, an invasion of even greater significance ensued in 1580, when Felipe II of Spain proclaimed himself king of Portugal and marched his armies across the border. The Spanish remained for another 60 years, during which time Madeira was a Spanish territory.

At the end of the 16th century, Madeira surrendered its domination of the sugar cane industry to another, much larger, Portuguese colony: Brazil. Sugar cane had taken a hefty toll on the Madeiran soil and the exhausted

Pirate treasure

The notorious English pirate Captain Kidd was hanged in London after terrorising the high seas for almost 10 years – but the loot he amassed was never found. Legend has it that his treasure is buried somewhere on the Ilhas Desertas, southeast of Madeira, although all searches so far have been fruitless.

Looe Rock and Funchal in the early 19th century

plantation soils were supplanted by less demanding grape vines. Although sugar cane is still grown today (for molasses and the brandy-like *aguardente*), it has long ceased to be Madeira's major crop.

Madeira and Britain

Britain's political and economic connections to Madeira can be traced to the 17th century. In 1662 Charles II married Portugal's Catherine of Bragança, and a provision written into the bride's dowry granted special favours to British settlers on Madeira. Both Madeira and Britain benefited from a new regulation that governed the shipment of Madeira wine and made it the only wine that could be exported directly to the British possessions in the Western hemisphere (all other wines had to be shipped to the Americas via a British harbour). Such trading rights attracted more Britons to the island, who founded dynastic families who, in some cases, still constitute the island's economic elite. Wine profits were huge, and by 1800 exports had reached 9 million bottles per year. Many of the grand country *quintas* (villas) that still dot the island today have their roots in the early Madeira wine industry.

British troops arrived on the island in 1801 to protect against possible invasion by the French, but they were withdrawn following the Treaty of Amiens in 1802. In 1807 the treaty was put in jeopardy and the troops returned, remaining until 1814. After the fall of Napoleon, many of the garrison remained and settled permanently on the island.

In Madeira, the second half of the 19th century was plagued by natural disaster. In 1852 the island's precious vines were blighted by mildew, wiping out an estimated 90 percent of the total crop. Just four years later, cholera claimed the lives of up to 7,000 Madeirans, and in 1872–3 the dreaded phylloxera louse destroyed the remainder of the vineyards. Potato and sugar crops were also badly affected.

Portugal took up arms during World War I, siding with the British and French. Madeira's strategic position for Atlantic

Celebrated Stopovers

Madeira, with its long tradition of hospitality, has welcomed many notable voyagers, including, in 1815, the defeated Napoleon Bonaparte. En route to exile on St Helena in the South Atlantic, Napoleon's ship anchored to take on supplies. The only visitor allowed aboard was the British consul, who graciously presented Britain's old enemy with bottles of vintage Madeira wine to help wile away his confinement – Napoleon responded with gold coins. History just about repeated itself after the 1974 coup, when the deposed Portuguese leaders, ex-President Tomás and Prime Minister Caetano, also stopped at Madeira en route to exile in Brazil. This time the defeated party was allowed ashore, but hospitality was less in evidence, and they were locked up in the São Lourenço fortress.

An *azulejo* frieze depicting a British tourist being carried by local men adorns Funchal's former Chamber of Commerce

shipping did not escape the notice of the German High Command, and in 1916 a German submarine bombarded Funchal harbour and sank three French ships.

Modern Times

As mainland Portugal lurched into a political and economic crisis that would bring down the country's republican government, many miles away Madeira was busy developing its tourist trade: the island had been a sought-after destination since the mid-19th century, attracting wealthy British sun-lovers, minor royalty and aristocrats from many countries. The celebrated Reid's Hotel had opened its doors in 1890, and a seaplane service started operating from Southampton in 1921. Madeira was awarded further cachet when the last of the Austro-Hungarian emperors, Charles I of Austria (also Charles IV of Hungary), chose Madeira as his home in exile after World War I. He died here in 1922 and his last resting place, in Monte's Nossa Senhora church, now receives a stream of pilgrims, following his beatification by Pope John Paul II in 2004.

In 1932 Portugal gained a new ruler, Dr António Salazar. His success at controlling inflation and reducing national debt made him a popular hero, but under the new ultra-conservative constitution of 1933 he effectively became dictator for life. Following a bloodless military coup in 1974, Salazar's successor, Dr Marcelo Caetano, was overthrown and free elections were held.

Two years later, Madeira was granted the status of Autonomous Political Region. A new island parliament would henceforth deal with all issues directly affecting Madeira, except defence, foreign affairs and tax, and for the first time Madeira was allowed to elect five members to the parliament in Lisbon.

In 1986 Portugal joined the European Economic Community (now the European Union). Generous funding from the EU has been invested in the island's fishing industry and infrastructure, such as roads, tunnels, marinas, leisure complexes and an expanded Funchal airport. When the EU money dried up, President Jardim turned to private investors to continue the building boom. Now some argue the island has gone from underdevelopment to overdevelopment, and in 2012, the tiny island found itself a startling €6 billion in debt.

Madeira appeals to tourists in a 1931 poster

Historical Landmarks

1351 A Genoese map depicts Madeira for the first time.

1418 Portuguese explorers discover Porto Santo.

1425 Madeira becomes a province of Portugal; sugar cultivation begins, followed by grapes and grain.

1478 Christopher Columbus briefly settles on the island.

1480 onwards Settlers arrive from Europe, including merchants who invest in the sugar plantations and irrigation systems.

1514 The population reaches 5,000. Funchal cathedral completed.

1566 Funchal sacked by French pirates; 300 islanders killed.

1580 Felipe II of Spain occupies Portugal; Madeira under Spanish rule.

1640 Portuguese regain their kingdom (and Madeira).

1703 Britain is granted valuable trade concessions with Portugal. Many Britons settle in Madeira and soon dominate the wine trade.

1801–14 Napoleon occupies Portugal; British troops stationed on Madeira.

1850 onwards European intellectuals and aristocrats 'discover' Madeira.

1872–3 Phylloxera destroys most of Madeira's vines. Bananas replace wine as the island's main cash crop.

1914–18 Portugal fights with the Allies in World War I. Funchal harbour bombarded by a German submarine.

1933–68 Salazar dictator of Portugal. Economic stagnation.

1939–45 Portugal neutral in World War II.

1960 Madeira's first airport, on Porto Santo.

1974 Bloodless revolution overthrows the dictatorship in Portugal.

1976 Madeira becomes an autonomous region with its own parliament.

1986 Portugal joins the EU; gets funds to improve Madeira's infrastructure.

1997 Via Rápida motorway opens, transforming island transport.

2001 The island's redeveloped airport allows large jets into Madeira.

2006 New theme parks and cable cars open around the island.

2010 Flash-floods cause a mud slide that kills 40 people.

2012 Madeira's debts are estimated at €6 billion.

2013 Wildfires whipped up by strong winds reach the Funchal suburb of Monte, destroying ten homes.

WHERE TO GO

GETTING AROUND

Madeira's size can be deceptive. At first glance it might seem that two days would be sufficient to see the whole 57 x 22km (35 x 13 miles). Indeed, it is possible to speed from Funchal to once-remote Porto Moniz in under an hour. But to do so means travelling mainly in tunnels. For a taste of the island's beautiful scenery, there is no alternative but to take to Madeira's mountainous terrain and winding, two-lane roads.

A minimum of three days is necessary to see a good portion of the island; a full week allows you to do it justice and take the time to enjoy its scenic outdoors at a relaxed pace. Many visitors are still advised to hop aboard day trip buses that take in the main attractions: although the roads have improved, travelling by car should only be undertaken by confident drivers who are comfortable negotiating steep, winding terrain.

More and more visitors are choosing to stay outside Funchal; the offer of mountain lodges and smaller coastal hotels has greatly improved over the years, and there are now visitors who barely set foot in the capital.

FUNCHAL

Funchal ❶ is the only town of any size on the island, indeed in the whole of the archipelago, and most of Madeira's historic buildings, museums and sights are located in the capital. With a population of around 110,000, it is a larger city than most expect to find on such a tiny island, but you can walk across

The mighty headland of Cabo Girão, on the western coast

Funchal and its harbour

the centre in just 10 to 15 minutes. Exploring inland to the north is difficult on foot, however: the streets become very steep. Nevertheless, walking remains the only practical way to see Funchal: the narrow, cobbled streets were never meant for vehicles, and they can be surprisingly congested with traffic, although some have now been pedestrianised.

One way to get your bearings upon arrival in Funchal is to walk out on the jetty known as the **Ilhéu de Pontinha** and view the city as those aboard cruise ships do. The Pontinha, which was built in 1962, leads round the container port and passes the old fortress (now a restaurant by day and disco by night), which is perched on top of what was once a tiny island known as Looe Rock.

Funchal's deep natural harbour propelled the city's development in the 15th and 16th centuries, when Madeira became known to those making expeditions to the Far East and the Americas. The busy port hosts cruise ships, yachts and picturesque (and functioning) fishing boats. The commercial freight Port of Caniçal is about 12 miles east of Funchal.

The Town Centre

The view of the town from the harbour is outstanding: squat white houses with terracotta roofs climb steeply through tropical greenery all around the spacious bay, with rugged mountains forming an attractive backdrop. The dominant building on the seafront is the **Palácio de São Lourenço** (Fortress of St Lawrence). Erected in the 16th century, it guarded the bay against pirates – you can see the ancient cannons poking through the crenellated walls. Walking up Avenida Zarco, past the main gate of the fort, you will see the white-gloved sentries who guard what is now the residence of Madeira's Prime Minister and the Military Command.

At the junction of Avenida Zarco and the main street, Avenida Arriaga, stands a statue of Madeira's discoverer, João Gonçalves Zarco – often referred to as the 'First Captain' – made in 1927 by Madeiran sculptor Francisco Franco, whose work can be seen all over the city. The imposing **Palácio do Governo Regional** Ⓐ, a handsome building with tiled patios and the administrative headquarters of Madeira, rises behind the Zarco monument to the right. Also on the right is the popular **Golden Gate Grand Café** whose pavement tables are excellent for people-watching, with a view of the cathedral (see page 31). Avenida Arriaga is particularly pretty in late spring, when the jacaranda trees are in full blossom.

Along here you will find the **tourist information office** and, next door at No. 28, the **Adegas de São Francisco** (The Old Blandy Wine Lodge; www.the oldblandywinelodge.com; Mon–Fri 10am–6.30pm, Sat 10am–1pm; guided tours can be booked online, charge), Madeira's oldest working

Palácio de São Lourenço

wine lodge. This atmospheric place was part of a Franciscan monastery, built in the 17th century. Here you can take a tour of the lodge to learn about the wine-making process, and visit the attics where fragrant wines mature in huge oak barrels. You don't need to take a tour to visit the handsome tasting room, decorated with frescoes painted by the German artist Max Römer, in 1922.

Just a few steps west of the lodge is the small **Jardim de São Francisco** (St Francis' Garden), a delightful urban green space with an open-air café set amid lush tropical vegetation. Across from the park is the **Teatro Municipal**, a miniature Victorian gem that hosts periodic concerts, plays and films. Across the road is the chic **Café Ritz**, an elegant café with regular live music. It was once the Chamber of Commerce and has fine *azulejo* (blue and white tile) vignettes that depict scenes from old Madeira.

Funchal's Sé (Cathedral) is one of the island's oldest buildings

Towards the centre, at the east end of Avenida Arriaga (at Rua João Tavira) is Funchal's principal landmark, the **Sé** **B** (Cathedral; Mon–Sat 9am–noon, 4–6pm; free). Begun in 1493 and completed in 1517, the cathedral is one of the few build-

ings in Funchal to survive from the early days of colonisation. The exterior is plain and simple, topped by a granite clock tower, but the cathedral's interior is lavish and impressive, lined with spectacular decoration. It has Gothic arches, a splendid inlaid cedar ceiling of Moorish design, beautifully carved blue and gold choir stalls, gilded altars and a sprinkling of nice *azulejos*.

Walking up Rua João Tavira, north of the cathedral, note the black and white mosaics paving the pedestrian shopping street, and explore the pretty narrow shopping streets to the right. At the top of Rua João Tavira is **Praça do Município** **C**, the town's dignified main square, with a huge fish-scale mosaic of black and white stones which gives the impression of an enormous chessboard, and historic buildings on all sides. On the northern side is the 17th-century **Igreja do Colégio** (Collegiate Church; Mon–Fri 9am–1pm, 3–6pm, Sat 4–6pm Sun 6–9pm; free), originally founded by the Jesuits in 1574. A spacious and airy old place, it is decorated with 17th- and 18th-century tiles, paintings and gilt woodcarving.

At the head of the square (east) stands the **Câmara Municipal** (Town Hall), which occupies a former 18th-century palace. Don't miss the graceful, 19th-century statue of *Leda and the Swan* in the inner courtyard. The statue used to be in the old fish market – a fact that is corroborated by the tiled panel outside the present municipal market (see page 35).

Volcanic stone is used to make mosaic pavements

On the square's south side is the **Museu de Arte Sacra** D (Museum of Religious Art; www.museuartesacra funchal.org; Tue–Sat 10am–12.30pm, 2.30–6pm, Sun 10am–1pm; charge). The museum is housed in a 17th-century palace, the former residence of the bishop of Funchal. The outstanding works on view include a dozen or so 15th- and 16th-century Flemish paintings, regarded as among the richest in Portugal and rare even in the rest of Europe. These vibrant masterpieces, as well as other excellent works from the Portuguese school of the same period, were donated to the island's churches by Madeira's wealthy sugar merchants, who during the 16th century traded their 'white gold' in Antwerp, which was then the home of a thriving artistic culture. There is also a fine collection of Flemish sculpture, as well as goldsmithery.

The main door of the museum leads to Rua do Bispo (Bishop Street) and both this and the parallel street, Rua Queimada Cima, are well worth exploring for their shops, cafés and historic buildings.

Continue west from the Praça do Municipio on Rua da Carreira, a bustling street full of popular old-fashioned shops and affordable restaurants. Left of here is the **Museu Fotographia Vicentes** (www.photographiamuseuvicentes. com.pt; Mon–Fri 10am–12.30pm, 2–5pm; charge) entered via a grand double staircase that sweeps up to the museum on the first floor from a plant-filled patio lined with cafés and shops. The photographs inside reflect 150 years of island life.

Further down the Rua da Carreira is the picturesque Rua da Mouraria, with antiques shops and the **Museu Municipal do Funchal** (Tue–Fri 10am–6pm, Sat–Sun noon–6pm; charge), another 18th-century aristocratic home converted into a museum. On the ground floor is a modest aquarium showing Madeira's sealife, while upstairs you will find an old-fashioned collection of stuffed local sea and land creatures.

At the top of the street is the charming **Igreja de São Pedro** (Mon–Sat 8am–noon, 5–7pm; free), built in the 16th century. Its walls are lined entirely with blue and white check-patterned *azulejos* and it has a beautifully painted wood ceiling, fine chandeliers, a massive gilded altar and side chapels.

About halfway up the steep Calçada de Santa Clara, at No. 7, you reach the **Casa Museu Frederico de Freitas** (Freitas House-Museum; Tue–Sun 10am–5.30pm; charge). It is divided into two parts: the modern wing is dedicated to *azulejos* and their history, while the old mansion alongside, the Casa de Calçada, is full of paintings of Madeira by 19th-century artists, and the furnishings of an affluent 19th-century household.

Stone Manueline window, Quinta das Cruzes

Continue uphill to the **Convento de Santa Clara** (Mon–Sat 10am–noon, 3–5pm; charge). Built towards the end of the 15th century and expanded two centuries later, it is now a school run by Franciscan nuns, but you can visit the convent and its church by ringing the bell by the convent gate. The church is a splendid building, with walls completely covered by rare 17th-century *azulejos* in geometric patterns, and with a fine painted ceiling. The ornate tomb at the back of the church is sometimes mistaken for that of Zarco, the island's discoverer; in fact it is the tomb of his son-in-law – Zarco's more humble grave lies beneath the modern timber floor of the high altar.

During his stint as governor of the island, Zarco lived a short way up Calçada do Pico, in the **Quinta das Cruzes** Ⓔ (Tue–Sun 10am–12.30pm, 2–5.30pm; charge). Constructed in the 15th century, but rebuilt after an earthquake in 1748 and expanded in the 19th century, this is Funchal's finest *quinta* (villa) open to the public. The main house is a museum of antiques: superb 16th-century Indo-Portuguese and 17th-century Madeiran as well as 18th- and 19th-century English pieces. The house is surrounded by a lovely, somewhat unkempt garden of exotic flowers, trees and plants (including a good orchid section). However, the outstanding feature is the 'archaeological garden', a display of relics from some of the oldest places on the island – tombstones, pieces taken from important buildings and two splendid early 16th-century stone Manueline windows.

Rua das Cruzes, the road separating Quinta das Cruzes from the convent, leads to a lookout point with a view over the town, the port and the dome of the English Church.

The Market, Old Town and Seafront

Between two *ribeiras* (river beds) that carry excess water from the mountains to the sea, is Rua Dr Fernão Ornelas, lined with

Stalls at the Mercado dos Lavradores

old shops, that leads to Funchal's central market. In spring, the little rivers are hidden beneath trellises of blazing bougainvillea. Directly ahead lies the **Mercado dos Lavradores** ❻ (Workers' Market; Mon–Thur 8am–7pm, Fri 7am–8pm, Sat 7am–2pm), housed in a two-storey, open-roofed structure built in 1937. The best time to visit is on Friday or Saturday, when fishermen, farmers and traders from all over the island pour into town. This is the only time when the central part is entirely filled with stalls. The market is bustling, fragrant and colourful, with fruit, vegetables and fish of all shapes, colours and sizes. Meat stalls can be found around the outside, as well as several wicker and handicraft shops.

The market marks the start of the **Zona Velha** ❼ (Old Town). The main streets are the narrow, cobbled alleyway of Rua de Santa Maria and, parallel, Rua Dom Carlos I. Once poor and decaying, but filled with character, this former fishermen's quarter has been transformed into a focus of tourist interest, with a seafront promenade, a cable-car station taking passengers up to the hill town of Monte (see page 41) and a popular attraction called the **Madeira Story Centre** (www.storycentre.com; daily 10am–6pm; charge), packed with exhibits, videos and interactive displays recounting the history of the island. The main focus of gentrification is the row of restaurants you reach at the pedestrian-only stretch at the eastern end, beyond which lies the **Capela do Corpo Santo** (Chapel of the Body of Christ; officially 10am–2pm, 3–5pm, but usually closed; free). The chapel, dating from the end of the 15th century, is one of the oldest in Funchal, built by a charity supporting the local fishermen. The low houses beyond once housed fishing families, but are gradually being taken over by artisans making leather sandals or selling lace and embroidery.

The view from the Fortaleza de São Tiago

At the far end of the Old Town is the **Fortaleza de São Tiago** (St James's Fortress). Built in the 17th century and expanded in the middle of the 18th, the picturesque fort now acts as a wonderful setting for the modest **Museu de Arte Contemporánea** (Museum of Contemporary Art; Mon–Fri 10am–12.30pm, 2–5pm; charge). There's an excellent restaurant in the fortress, with views along the steep cliffs that rise to the east of Funchal.

Back on the seafront, heading west, is the **Parlamento Regional**, with a modern debating chamber. Behind it is the **Alfândega Velha** (Old Customs House), built in the 16th century. Two blocks west, on Praça do Colombo, the **Museu a Cidade do Açúcar** (City of Sugar Museum; normally Mon–Fri 10am–12.30pm, 2–6pm, but closed at the time of writing; charge) tells the story of the island's 15th-century sugar trade.

> ### Niemeyer's work
>
> The architect of the striking Pestana Casino Park hotel was the Brazilian, Oscar Niemeyer. He also designed the adjoining casino, which is built in the shape of a giant crown of thorns.

West of Town

Avenida Arriaga ends at the Praça do Infante, where a statue of Prince Henry the Navigator sits at the easternmost tip of **Parque Santa Catarina** 🅗 (St Catherine's Park; daily Apr–Sept 7am–9pm, Oct–Mar 8am–7pm; free). A delightful hilltop retreat, this park has splendid views over the marina. Aside from the gardens, lake and playground, other points of interest include several bronze statues (including *The Sower* by Francisco Franco, dating from 1923); and the Chapel of Santa Catarina, said to be the island's oldest chapel (permanently locked). At the west end of the park, the elegant pink **Quinta Vigia** is the residence of Madeira's civil governor.

Above the park looms the startling sight of the Pestana Casino Park hotel. The giant box of a hotel signals the start of the traditional hotel zone, flush with well-known, de luxe 5-star hotels such as the Savoy (under refurbishment; no completion date as yet), the Pestana Carlton and Reid's, plus a few 4-star hotels, *quintas* and posh restaurants.

West of Reid's is the *Zona Turista*. Stretching for 3km (2 miles) along the clifftops east of the city, this includes numerous fine hotels and resort complexes and, at the far end, the huge Forum Madeira shopping centre. Not all is brash consumerism, however: a delightfully landscaped sea-front promenade extends eastwards for 2km (1 mile), with children's play areas, swimming pools, cafés and well-tended gardens.

Glorious Gardens

A short bus or taxi ride into the hillsides northeast of Funchal (on the road to Camacha) takes you to the wonderful **Jardim Botânico** ❶ (Botanical Garden; daily

Clifftop Palace

Standing high over Funchal harbour is Reid's, one of the world's most famous hotels. It was begun by William Reid, a Scot who arrived in Madeira aged 14 in 1836, having run away to sea. He became a prosperous wine merchant in Funchal and by the age of 25 was also renting and managing *quintas* for well-to-do invalids from northern Europe. Some of these villas he converted into hotels, and in due course he acquired the clifftop site for the luxury hotel of his dreams. He died before it could be finished, and the project was completed by his sons Willy and Albert. Reid's finally opened its doors in 1891. In 1937 the hotel passed into the hands of the Blandy family, another famous British-Madeiran dynasty, and in 1996 it was acquired by the Orient-Express group, which has refurbished it without sacrificing any of its fin de siècle grandeur, and restored its original name, Reid's Palace. It remains the epitome of upper-class luxury, and eminent guests over the years have included Sir Winston Churchill, Charles I of Austria, General Batista of Cuba, and the writer George Bernard Shaw, who signed up for dancing lessons here at the grand age of 71.

9am–6pm; charge), the most comprehensive public garden on the island. A wonderland for any plant-lover, the gardens have examples of virtually every plant that grows on Madeira and lots of subtropical flowers and plants from far-flung destinations. It occupies steep terraces that offer fine views over Funchal.

The adjacent **Jardim dos Loiros** (Bird Park) has been incorporated into the Botanical Garden and contains all manner of tropical

Formal gardens at the Jardim Botânico

birds. Uphill from the Botanical Garden, the **Teleféricos do Jardim Botânico** (Botanical Garden Cable Car; www.telefericojardimbotanico.com; daily Apr–Sept 9.30am–5.30pm, Oct–Mar 9am–5pm; charge) offers the chance to glide high above the green ravine west of the Botanical Garden up to the hilltown of Monte (see page 41). It is a fantastic trip.

Orchid lovers might like to head in the opposite direction, along the steep downhill walk to the **Jardim Orquídea** (Pregetter's Orchid Garden; www.madeira-orchid.com; daily 9am–6pm; charge). This orchid-breeding project has some 50,000 plants and more than 4,000 varieties of the delicate, finely coloured blooms.

Another garden dedicated to orchids, on the eastern side of the city, is the **Quinta da Boa Vista** (Rua Luis Figueiroa de Albuquerque; Mon–Sat 9am–5.30pm; charge), set in the grounds of a beautiful 200-year-old villa. This is a busy working

The luxuriant Palheiro Gardens

orchid farm, founded in the 1960s, which has received numerous awards, most notably from the British Royal Horticultural Society.

But the most splendid of Madeira's horticultural wonders are without doubt the **Palheiro Gardens** **J** (Mon–Fri 9am–4.30pm; charge).

The hillside estate, only a short bus ride from Funchal to the east of the city, is the property of the family that once owned Reid's Hotel (see page 38) and is one of the famous producers of Madeira wine. Built in the 1820s, the *quinta* has been in the hands of the Blandy family for more than a century. The gardens are styled rather like an English country garden, and are famous for their winter-flowering camellias, though the diversity of exotic plants, including a lush array of tropical species, ensures stunning displays throughout the year. The long, cobbled entrance avenue is shaded by plane trees, while the fields that lie on either side are carpeted with a wonderful spread of arum and belladonna lilies in spring, and agapanthus in summer and autumn.

Formal and informal areas are landscaped with pools and fountains, while terraces tumble down the hillsides. A deep, wild ravine with thick tropical vegetation is nicknamed the 'Valley of Hell'. Yet the garden retains the distinctive, charming and peaceful atmosphere of the timeless grounds of an English country house.

AROUND FUNCHAL

A number of excellent visits are within easy reach of Funchal. Tour operators often promote Monte, Camacha and Curral das Freiras as a popular half-day excursion.

Monte

The hilltop town of **Monte ❷** has been fashionable ever since wealthy merchants and exiled aristocrats in the 19th century built their splendid *quintas* up here in the cool air above Funchal. Today it is perhaps best known for the toboggan

Downhill Racers

Monte's famous wicker toboggans were used at the beginning of the 19th century to carry freight down the frighteningly steep 5km (3-mile) hill between Monte and Funchal. A British merchant, living in Monte and weary of winding his way down to Funchal every day, hit on the idea that the same toboggans could carry people. A wicker seat was fixed to the basic sled and so the *carros de cesto* (literally basket-cars) were born. Each *carro* is controlled by two *carreiros*, complete with traditional straw boaters, who give an initial push and then ride along until another push, or pull, or sudden brake, is required, depending on the desired speed and any traffic ahead. For brakes they use the rubber soles of their boots.

The modern toboggan ride (Mon–Sat 9am–6pm) is but a pale shadow of its former self (even though the fare of €25 for one person, €30 for two, is worthy of a high-tech roller-coaster). The road surface is no longer the friction-free, slippery cobbles that once had *carros* careering down the hill. Toboggans now slide more slowly than they used to. The lot of the *carreiros* has also improved, even if their outfits remain traditional. They used to have to walk back up the hill, carrying or pushing the 68kg (150lb) sleds, but nowadays they do the journey by truck.

Transport by wicker toboggan

rides that originate here, though the toboggans now have a rival in the form of the cable cars that link Monte with the Jardim Botânico (see page 38) and to Funchal's Old Town (Teleféricos da Madeira; www.telefericodofunchal.com; daily 9am–5.45pm; charge).

Monte's main square is on the western side of the town, and is a pleasant evocation of yesteryear. The rack-and-pinion railway that once laboured up the ferociously steep hill closed in the 1930s, but the railway station is still here on the western side of the tree-shaded square, and the viaduct arches now rise over the perfectly clipped public gardens of the **Jardim do Monte** (established 1894).

A short walk up a path from the square is the elegant and richly decorated **Igreja de Nossa Senhora do Monte** (Our Lady of Monte), dedicated to Madeira's patron saint. On the Feast of the Assumption, 15 August, thousands make the annual pilgrimage to the church. Others come throughout the year to pray at the chapel on the left of the church that holds the tomb of the last of the Austro-Hungarian emperors, Charles I of Austria (and IV of Hungary), who died in Madeira in 1922, and whose path to sainthood was prepared when he was beatified by Pope John Paul II in 2004. At the foot of the church steps is the starting point of the **Carrinhos de Monte** – the ride down the hill aboard a wicker toboggan (see page 41).

The **Jardim do Palácio do Monte** (Monte Palace Tropical Gardens; www.montepalace.com; daily 9.30am–6pm; charge), a short walk east of the church, is firmly rooted in the past. The gardens that surround the château-like Monte Palace – once the area's most fashionable hotel – are home to hundreds of plants and various other displays. They are lushly beautiful, and within the gates is an impressive collection of native and exotic flora (especially good cycads), a koi pond, a porcelain collection and historical artefacts from throughout Portugal, including architectural pieces taken from important buildings and prized *azulejo* panels. The unimpeded views of Funchal are unbeatable.

But in Monte one is spoiled for choice when it comes to fine gardens. There is another situated above the cable-car terminus, forming the grounds of the **Quinta do Monte** hotel. Visitors are welcome to explore the well-tended terrace gardens (www.quintadomontemadeira.com; free) and take coffee or lunch in the delightful garden pavilion. The last garden is that of the villa in which the Emperor Charles I spent the brief months of his exile in Madeira. The **Quinta Jardins do Imperador** (Mon–Sat 9am–5.30pm; charge) lies on the western side of the town square, along Caminho do Pico.

Terreiro da Luta, at 876m (2,873ft), has its base about 1.5km (1 mile) north of Monte, but climbs another 330m (1,080ft) to the top and offers another magnificent panorama of Funchal. It was here that the figure of Our Lady of Monte

Curral das Freiras, the Refuge of the Nuns

(now in the church below) was allegedly discovered in the 15th century. On the summit is a monument to Nossa Senhora da Paz (Our Lady of Peace), dedicated to the end of World War I. Around the monument are anchor chains from French ships sunk in Funchal harbour by German torpedoes.

Villages in the Hills

A good half-day excursion by bus, taxi or organised tour is the 16km (10-mile) trip north on the narrow, twisting road to **Curral das Freiras ❸** (Refuge of the Nuns), a village that has been isolated from the outside world for the majority of its history, a perfect crater surrounded by extinct volcanoes. The nuns in question fled here from Santa Clara Convent in the 16th century to escape raiding pirates. Protected on all sides – hidden would be more accurate – by inaccessible mountains, and supported by rich volcanic soil and abundant sunshine, their settlement became permanent.

The village became famous for its cherries and chestnuts, and the popular liqueurs made from those products: *ginja* and *licor de castanha*; the cakes here are also excellent. The village continued in splendid isolation until the 20th century, when tunnels were bored through the mountains to bring the first roads. Television finally reached the village in 1986.

Curral das Freiras is nice enough, but its whitewashed houses with terracotta roofs are best seen from above. The view from the lookout point of **Eira do Serrado** (1,006m/3,300ft) is breathtaking. If you opt for a bus tour, make sure a stop at Eira do Serrado is included (there is also great shopping and an *estalagem*, or inn, here). An alternative view is from the south, across the valley, at the lookout point **Boca dos Namorados** (Lovers' Nest). This is a difficult trek, which, although feasible by car, is usually incorporated on Jeep safari itineraries. From here, the panorama sweeps round and takes in the entire valley (though even at 1,100m/3,608ft you will still be close enough to hear the bell of the village church).

In the opposite direction, 16km (10 miles) northeast of Funchal, is **Camacha**, a pretty village at nearly 700m (2,300ft). In the heart of willow country, it is the island's centre of the wickerwork industry. Many of the local inhabitants are employed crafting furniture, table mats, baskets and other household items. Around Camacha and north of here you are likely to see

Around 2,000 of Camacha's population work with wicker

the stripped willow soaked and left to dry, either by a river-bank, propped up against a house, or in wigwam fashion in the fields. You may even see families at the roadside, soaking the willow in vats and stripping off the bark. Most weaving is done at home – the only place you are guaranteed to see artisans at work is at Café Relógio (a wickerwork factory and café-restaurant complex). The upstairs restaurant has panoramic views, while the downstairs is a 'wicker super-store'. Camacha is also the starting point for two excellent *levada* walks heading west to Vale do Paraíso and northeast to Eira de Fora. To enjoy these walks without getting lost, you need a walking guidebook, such as the ultra-reliable Walk & Eat Madeira *Sunflower* guide, available in shops all over the island (see page 124).

WESTERN MADEIRA

Western Madeira begins just beyond the capital's tourist zone. Here, the pace is slower and the coast even less discovered than further east. Inland is some glorious countryside.

The lighthouse at Ponta do Pargo, the island's western tip

Câmara de Lobos and Cabo Girão

Just 8.5km (5.3 miles) west of Funchal is **Câmara de Lobos** ❹ (Lair of the Sea-wolves). The peculiar name refers to the seals that once swam near here. Câmara de Lobos is more picturesque from afar than it is up close. In 1950, Winston Churchill spent time on the island painting the fishing port,

Picturesque Câmara de Lobos is still an active fishing village

an interest that ensured its standing as an idyllic, old-world fishing village. The gaily-painted boats are still here, as is the protected, natural rocky harbour.

The port area has resisted attempts at gentrification and fairly swaggers with macho atmosphere. Hard-drinking locals down *poncha* (sugar cane brandy, lemon juice and honey) in shadowy bars, while grizzled old fishermen play cards or repair their boats. Close to the waterfront is the small Fishermen's Chapel, an early 15th-century project that was later rebuilt (1723), and where locals give thanks for the villagers' safe return from the sea. Otherwise, there's not much for the tourist here, but you have to hand it to Câmara de Lobos for remaining a pure and simple working port.

Beyond Câmara de Lobos, the coastal road climbs for 8km (5 miles), also dipping inland, passing through rich agricultural country, famous for the high quality of its grapes. Eventually it leads to the top of the mighty headland known as **Cabo Girão ⑤**. One of the highest cliffs in the world, it plummets 590m (1,900ft) to the Atlantic. The views east and west along the coast are sensational. There's a terrifying, exhilarating viewpoint, where you stand on a glass floor, clutching a glass-panelled rail, with nothing else beneath you save the sweep of the wild sea hundreds of metres below. Agapanthus cling to the top of the promontory, and pine and eucalyptus creep right to the edge, but an even greater degree of daring can be seen hundreds of metres below, where farmers have managed to salvage tiny plots of arable land, terracing them on the sides and base of the cliff.

The winding road continues on through the sprawling settlements of Quinta Grande and Campanário. The latter, an important grape-growing area, is also remarkable for its cliff-side caves, used by local fishermen for storage purposes.

Ribeira Brava

The next major settlement, heading west, is **Ribeira Brava ⑥**. If you are in a hurry, it can be reached in just 20 minutes on the *via rápida* highway from Funchal. The town's name, which means 'wild river' or 'wild ravine', seems hyperbolic for such an orderly and peaceful little community. Except in winter, Ribeira Brava's river is more of a tame trickle. The river heads due north, as does the road – straight across the island (a mere 20km/12 miles) to São Vicente – making the ancient town of Ribeira Brava (established in 1440) an important junction.

The main focus of attention is the 16th-century **São Bento** (St Benedict's church), with some of the island's finest gilded and carved woodwork, a nativity and an elaborate font. In Rua de São Francisco, the **Museu Etnográfico da Madeira** (Madeira Ethnographic Museum; Tue–Fri 9.30am–5pm, Sat–Sun 10am–12.30pm, 1.30–5.30pm; charge) is an excellent introduction to the fishing, farming and wine-making

Bananas are big business along the south coast of Madeira

traditions that still just about survive in Madeira's more remote outposts.

The Southwest Coast

From Ribeira Brava, most coach excursions head north to São Vicente (see page 52), as the road cuts through some of the best scenery on the whole island. However, those with more time can continue along the southwest coast.

Ponta do Sol is the next village after Ribeira Brava. As its name suggests, it is blessed with more than its fair share of sunshine. Only during the summer does it really come alive, however, when beach umbrellas are set out on the seafront lido. There are two buildings of note here: an 18th-century church and an arts centre, the **John dos Passos Cultural Centre**, housed in the restored home of the American novelist's grandparents, who emigrated from this village in the mid-19th century.

About 10km (6 miles) west of Ponta do Sol is **Calheta ❼**, a banana plantation centre and the only town of significance as you head west. The Igreja Matriz, the parish church, dates from 1430 but was rebuilt in 1639, and features a handsome Moorish-style ceiling. Next door is the Engenho da Calheta, a sugar mill, which produces honey and rum. Calheta has been the beneficiary of substantial tourism investment, with a large artificial-sand beach, and the **Casa das Mudas Arts Centre**, located on the clifftop to the west of the town – well worth visiting for its bold Modernist architecture, as well as for an adventurous programme of contemporary art exhibitions, and a cinema showing arthouse films.

From Calheta, a steep inland road climbs to the very centre of the island, up to the **Paúl da Serra ❽** (High Moorland). This plateau measures some 17 x 6km (11 x 3.5 miles), and the flat plain stands in dramatic contrast to the rugged mountains elsewhere on Madeira. The scenery is reminiscent of the moors of Scotland, and can be bleak, but on clear days it is possible to see both the north and south coasts of the island. In good weather, hikers are drawn to its remote and barren character. If you are thinking of hiking here, be warned that mists descend suddenly; you may want to go with a guide (see page 119).

The scenic 25 Fontes

Where the road from Calheta joins the main road across the moorland, turn right for the large car park that serves **Rabaçal ❾**, a beautiful valley popular among Madeirans at weekends and holidays. This is the starting point for a couple of spectacular *levada* walks.

Natural swimming pools in the volcanic rock at Porto Moniz

Both involve walking downhill from the car park along the narrow and twisting tarmac road that leads to the resthouse and barbecue pits at Rabaçal, then following the signs. The trip to the **Risco waterfall** is flat and takes about 30 minutes there and back. The other takes about three hours and involves a pretty steep climb along the way to **25 Fontes** (25 Springs)–as the name suggests, a verdant and water-filled spot. Both walks, indicated on almost all maps of Madeira, are wonderfully scenic.

The Northwest Coast

At the island's extreme northwestern tip is **Porto Moniz** ⑩, 75km (46 miles) from Funchal via the coastal road (only 50km/30 miles across the island), but it seems a world away. A tongue of volcanic lava flowed into the Atlantic thousands of years ago; it cooled and was carved by the sea into a series of protected natural pools. Small plots of land,

Waterfall near Seixal

divided by heath-tree fencing (to protect crops from the salt-laden wind) climb the hills overlooking the sea. You could spend a happy hour or two here, especially if the weather is warm and you want to paddle in rock pools or sit on the volcanic rocks and contemplate the ocean. There are several restaurants selling fish and seafood.

East from here, the dramatic **coastal road** is one of the island's star attractions. The original road (signposted Antiga 101 – Old 101), carved into the cliff in 1950, is a one-way route that can only be driven east to west (from São Vicente to Porto Moniz). Driving the other way on the coastal road you will catch a glimpse of this old corniche road, literally set on a ledge cut into the cliff face. As you depart Porto Moniz, you will pass a rocky outcrop with a hole carved into it like an open window; this has lent its name to the nearest settlement, **Ribeira da Janela** (Valley of the Window). After rain, you might also see water gushing down from the mountains and forming waterfalls.

Seixal ⓫ ('say-shall') is the only other settlement before São Vicente. The Sercial grape, used to produce the driest style of Madeira, grows on impossible-seeming steep terraces behind this coastal village, protected from wind and salt-laden air by bracken fences.

São Vicente ⓬, perhaps the prettiest village on the island, begins at the point where the northern coastal road meets the north–south road heading 21km (13 miles) to Ribeira Brava. The town lies just south of an unusual little chapel carved out of a rock. São Vicente's compact, well-kept centre is pedestrian-only, and attractive shops and cafés look onto Igreja Matriz, a lovely church with a painted ceiling depicting St Vincent. Tourism is making inroads, and a few restaurants have been designed with day-trippers in mind, but the village remains pristine – it is set inland, protected from the harsh ocean winds.

The **Grutas e Centro do Vulcanismo** (Caves and Vulcanology Centre; tel: 291-842 404; daily 10am–7pm; charge) are on the opposite side of the river from the village. Formed when a now-extinct volcano erupted more than 400,000 years ago, the caves were carved by molten lava. The 'tubes' formed are more than 1km (0.6 miles) in length. In 1855 an Englishman discovered the caves, which, being a lava bed,

São Vicente, one of Madeira's most attractive villages

Changeable weather

Madeira is known for its microclimates. Even though it's a small island, the weather can change several times over the course of the day, or if you move just 5km (3 miles). Clouds come and go with great alacrity, so don't despair if a day starts overcast – the clouds may clear in a matter of minutes.

do not have icy limestone stalagmites and stalactites but 'lava drops' that look like thick whirls of chocolate mousse. In a low-rise building near the cave entrance is an exhibition centre with some technical displays on volcanic processes and the island's geology, but also some enjoyable audio visuals showing how Madeira and its neighbouring islands were formed by the combination of volcanic eruption and the erosive effects of wind and rain.

High on a hill above the village is an odd church – actually a clockless clock tower – standing over a small chapel dedicated to Our Lady of Fátima. This isolated spot is a significant pilgrimage site, and can be seen for kilometres around.

From here, the road tunnels through the mountains back to Ribeira Brava, but the old road continues to cut its way upwards through verdant countryside until finally coming to a crest at the pass of **Boca da Encumeada** (626m/2,054ft). From here you can see right to the north coast and well into the south, while on each side are vast expanses of mountain scenery. This is one of the starting points for treks to Pico Ruivo, which is the highest peak on the island (1,862m/6,109ft).

One of the best *levada* walks on the island skirts the edge of the mountain and takes in the entire valley, with views of the sea. Look for the steps opposite the Bar-Restaurant Encumeada. The walk along the irrigation canal is lined with hydrangeas and ferns. It's around a 45-minute walk until you reach a second tunnel. From here you can return to follow Levada das Rabaças, for more amazing views.

About 3km (1.5 miles) south of the pass, perched on the edge of Serra de Água, is a handsome and comfortable mountain chalet, the best of its kind on Madeira, and the only pousada on the island – the **Pousada dos Vinháticos** (a *vinhático* is a type of Madeiran mahogany tree) with fabulous mountain views. It is the perfect place for lunch on the terrace, but many visitors, especially those with hiking on their minds, find it an ideal place to stay several days.

The valley on the opposite side of the road, south of the *pousada*, is known as **Serra de Água** and was the island's first hydroelectric power station (Madeira now has four). In spite of the modern technology, the valley remains a quiet agricultural community tucked away in some of the island's lushest hills.

The road from here leads down into Ribeira Brava, where the *via rápida* motorway whisks you back to Funchal.

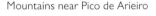
Mountains near Pico de Arieiro

Climbers reach the summit of Pico Ruivo

THE CENTRAL HIGHLANDS

The rugged mountain range that splits the island into north and south makes weather forecasting difficult in Madeira. While it is usually warm and clear down in Funchal, the mountains are often shrouded in a wintry mist. But this doesn't necessarily mean that you will have no view once you start climbing. Mountain tops often jut through the clouds, a spectacular sight in itself. Madeira's microclimates are hard to judge, especially from below. If it looks clear, beat a hasty path up to Pico do Arieiro first thing in the morning. By the time you get to Poiso you should know whether the journey will be worth the effort.

To see a particularly picturesque section of this terrain, drive north (and uphill) from Funchal towards Santana on the north coast on the ER103. There are beautiful vistas, secluded villages and a range of exhilarating walks en route.

Pico do Arieiro

At 1,818m (5,900ft), **Pico do Arieiro** ⓭ is Madeira's third-highest mountain, and its summit is reachable by car. As the road rises, the rugged countryside becomes spectacularly barren, though plunging volcanic hillsides have been softened and greened by time.

The lookout point at the windswept, Mars-like summit provides a 360-degree panorama. With its stratified canyon walls, a field of frozen lava and rust-red boulders, it's a geologist's dream. During summer, the terrain is parched, while at other times it is often covered with snow. The overnight temperature plunges below freezing most of the year, while the average annual temperature is below 10°C (50°F). There is also six times as much rain here as in Funchal. If the arrival of clouds catches you unaware, take refuge in the café on the summit.

At 1,862m (6,109ft), **Pico Ruivo**, the 'rooftop of Madeira', is only fractionally higher than Pico do Arieiro, but much less accessible. The peak can be reached by a walk of approximately one hour from Achada do Teixeira in the north, or the classic but strenuous four-hour round-trip hike from Pico do Arieiro. The latter is well signposted and there is a paved footpath, with drops protected by railings. The trek is popular; on a good day you will see several other walkers, so don't worry about losing your way. Warm clothing and hiking boots are essential, though, and in winter bear in mind that conditions on the mountains can be hazardous, with landslides removing parts of the path as well as icy winds and slippery mud. If you suffer from vertigo it is best not to even attempt the walk.

Ribeiro Frio and the Levada Trails

Back on the main road north (past Poiso) is the enchanting **Ribeiro Frio** ⓮, more a bend in the road than a town. Though the name means Cold River, it is a sunny and sheltered spot. If it happens to be cold or wet, pop into Restaurante Ribeiro

Following a *levada* trail

Frio, which resembles an Alpine chalet, warming visitors with log fires and freshly grilled trout from the hatchery across the road. You may have to wait to be served, as it's a very popular choice. Adjacent to the restaurant is a tiny chapel and a small botanical garden.

The trout hatchery is a series of interconnected concrete pools; the trout become increasingly large as you go along the pools. The botanical garden is not in the same league as the beautiful gardens in Funchal, but it nevertheless claims to have examples of every native species of flower, plant and tree to be found in Madeira, and sprawls unpredictably along twisting paths among shady trees.

Ribeiro Frio is relaxing, but its popularity is due to the two **walks** that begin here. The shorter one covers 2km (1 mile) to the outstanding lookout point known as the **Balcões** (Balconies), and takes just 45 minutes there and back. After a stroll through the woods, you reach a series of platforms that seem suspended in mid-air, with stupendous views across steep hillsides and dramatic ravines to the distinctive peaks of Ruivo and Arieiro. If it's not hidden in cloud cover, the sight certainly ranks as one of the most beautiful on the island. The second walk is one of the island's most popular *levada* trails (see page 119). This circular walk continues for around 7km (4.3 miles). Follow the signs for Portela and then walk along the Levada do Furado, turning right along the Levada do Bezerro. You will then cross the plateau Chão das Feiteiras before returning to Ribeiro Frio. An alternative, longer walk is to continue on the Levada do Furado until it reaches **Portela**. This walk takes most people about three hours, so you may wish to arrange for a taxi to collect you at Portela.

The Road to Santana

North of Ribeiro Frio, towards the coast, is **Faial**, set picturesquely at the foot of the Penha d'Águia (Eagle Rock). There is little of note in the village itself, aside from a handsome church and the Casa de Chá do Faial (Faial Tea Room) – actually a restaurant, with picture windows and fine rooftop panoramas. The road winds west past several good lookout points for fine views of the village from the main road.

Santana ⓱ is home to an enchantingly picture-book style of housing – A-framed structures known as *palheiros* (very

Levada Trails

Few man-made things on Madeira can rival its natural gifts. *Levadas* – simple irrigation channels that provide direct access to the best of the island's natural beauty – offer the best of both worlds. Cut no more than 50cm (20 ins) wide, and set 30–60cm (1–2ft) into the ground, *levadas* run more than 2,100km (1,300 miles) around Madeira and have been here almost as long as the island has been settled. The footpaths alongside each *levada* were built for maintenance purposes, but they create a great network for exploring the interior of the island. Some *levadas* are suitable for people of all ages; the only requirements are reasonable footwear, a reliable guidebook (such as the *Sunflower* guide, see page 124) and, at most, a taxi waiting at the other end. As *levadas* wind through the hillsides, most gradients are gentle, but paths that follow the lie of the hillside can also give rise to unexpected vertiginous drops.

similar to the A-framed cow huts that dot the hillsides around the town). The classic *palheiro* is a two-storey white stucco house with a brightly painted red door, red and blue window-frames and shutters and, essentially, a thatched roof. Two *palheiros*, perfectly painted in red, white and blue, are the objects of many tourist cameras because they are located in the centre of the village (one houses a tourist information centre).

Another *palheiro* that you can explore is in the grounds of the the the north **Parque Temático do Madeira** (Madeira Theme Park; www.parquetematicodamadeira.pt; mid-June–mid-Sept & mid-Dec–mid-Jan daily 10am–7pm, Jan–mid-June and mid-Sept–mid-Dec Tue–Sun; charge). Set in 3 hectares (7 acres) of land, this is one of Madeira's best attractions for children, with rock-climbing walls, adventure playgrounds and a boating lake, plus some good displays on the ecology, history, customs and landscape of the Madeiran islands.

Thatched houses of a larger, more conventional kind are to be found 5km (3 miles) south of Santana, in **Queimadas**, a complex of cottage-style rest houses with attractive gardens, set in the midst of Unesco-listed forest. It's a lovely spot for a picnic, although if the weather is clear you might take the opportunity to ascend to the island's pinnacle. This is reached by a 10km (6-mile) drive south of Santana, through the forest park of Pico das Pedras, up to **Achada do Teixeira** at 1,592m (5,223ft). From here, it is a two-hour round-trip walk to Pico Ruivo (see page 57).

The scenery northwest of Santana is just as delightful. **São Jorge** has a richly ornamented historic church, while past the village there is a splendid panorama from the *miradouro* at **Cabanas**, over to the valley of Arco de São Jorge.

The road winds inland towards the picturesque, fertile countryside around **Fajã do Penedo** and on to the pretty village of **Boaventura**. To cool off in a seafront lido, follow the coast road down to the small peninsula of **Ponta Delgada**,

Santana's unusual *palheiros* are unique to the area

where the church next to the lido has a flamboyant ceiling painting depicting biblical stories. From here it's just 5km (3 miles) to São Vicente, at which point the road heads south to Ribeira Brava, then east back to Funchal.

EASTERN MADEIRA

The eastern section of Madeira is not as mountainous as the centre, but it has some wonderful coastal spots, a handful of attractive small towns, productive agricultural fields and a long, surreal promontory that juts out into the Atlantic.

As you head out of Funchal, the village of **Santo da Serra** 16 can be reached via Camacha or from the Poiso crossroads. The altitude of 670m (2,200ft) produces refreshing breezes, and explains why several wealthy British expats have chosen to build *quintas* here and why so many affluent Madeirans still flee the Funchal summer up into these hills.

Ponta de São Lourenço

The most striking feature of Santo da Serra is its flatness; it may not be in the league of Paúl da Serra, but it is still large enough to accommodate a 27-hole golf course (see page 87). Even if you're not much of a golfer, you might still enjoy a stroll through the pleasant gardens of **Quinta da Junta**, once owned by the ubiquitous Blandy family, but now open to the public. A lookout point provides views across to Machico on the coast, and you can enjoy a drink at the golf club bar, set in what was once a *pousada*.

At **Portela** (662m/2,172ft), the views of the coast are striking. You may see hang-gliders taking off from a nearby platform. **Penha d'Águia** dominates the northeast coast. This huge rock formation, towering at 590m (1,935ft), levels off to a flat top. The name, meaning Eagle Rock, is derived from the eagles that once nested on ledges in its craggy cliff face.

The village of **Porto da Cruz**, 6km (4 miles) north, lies in the shadow of the rock. Here you will find one of Madeira's few sugar mills still working, pumping out steam as it processes the sugar cane to make *aguardente*, the local liquor, and molasses, which you can buy here.

Machico

Machico ⑰ is Madeira's first settlement, the spot where João Gonçalves Zarco first came ashore in 1419. Zarco ruled the southwestern half of Madeira, while his fellow Portuguese captain and navigator, Tristão Vaz Teixeira, governed the northeastern half from Machico. A statue of Teixeira stands outside the town's 15th-century parish church, **Igreja Matriz**. King Manuel I donated the statue of the Virgin (over the altar) and the distinguished church portal. The latter is a fine example of the exuberant style of Manueline architecture.

From Machico's triangular 'square', several streets lead to the beautifully landscaped seafront, home to a small custard-yellow fortress, built in 1706 and now used as the tourist information centre. Its battered walls contrast starkly with the ultramodern glass and concrete **Fórum Machico** cultural centre nearby. This exciting contemporary building has an inexpensive first-floor café and a ground-floor restaurant with panoramic views of Machico's wide bay. To the right, as you face the sea, is the tiny 18th-century **Capela de São Roque**, while the modern suspension bridge on the left of the bay leads to the **Capela dos Milagres** (Chapel of Miracles) built over the graves of Robert Machim and Anne d'Arfet, the first to set foot on Madeira (see page

A Madeira stonecrop plant

16). Beyond the chapel, the town's former boatyard is now a picturesque marina, with shops and cafés.

The Northeast Coast

The landscape of the extreme eastern peninsula, known as **Ponta de São Lourenço**, is more like Porto Santo (see page 66) and the Ilhas Desertas (see page 11) than Madeira. Keen walkers enjoy this wild, windswept tip of the island but, for all its wonderful views, it can be a bit too invigorating for comfort.

Close by, at **Prainha**, is the island's only natural sandy beach. Not surprisingly for a volcanic island, the sand here is black; the tiny beach can be crowded in high summer, but is deserted the rest of the year.

Nearby **Caniçal** ⓲ was once a whaling port, but since whaling was banned here in 1981, all that remains of this formerly lucrative industry is a museum and souvenirs on sale around the town. Although the **Museu da Baleia** (Whale Museum; tel: 291-961 858; www.museudabaleia.org; Tue–Sun 10am–6pm; charge) shows a video of a local whale hunt from 1978, the owner is the epitome of a poacher-turned-gamekeeper. Once commander of the Caniçal whaling station and thus responsible for taking 100–200 of the

Whale Museum, Caniçal

great creatures each year, he now devotes his energy to saving the whale and other marine life of the area. The 14m (45ft) model of the sperm whale is a reminder of the leviathans that once swam in great schools in the waters off Madeira. Whales are still sighted here, but not frequently. Caniçal is still a working fishing port, and has a selection of good fish restaurants.

Journeying back to Funchal from Caniçal via Machico, you will encounter the international airport, the **Aeroporto de Santa Catarina**, which serves the whole of Madeira. As you continue driving east, you actually travel underneath the runway, which is supported on huge pillars – a novel, if sobering, sensation.

Beyond the airport is the pleasant town of **Santa Cruz 19**, with an attractive church dating from the 16th century. Across the main square, the town hall retains

Mural, Santa Cruz market hall

a pair of splendid 15th- to 16th-century Manueline windows. A few streets away, the courthouse is another historic survivor, with fine verandas and an impressive main staircase. Along the seafront is the modern municipal market and a pebbly beach, while to the west of the town is the island's only waterpark, the **Aquaparque** (http://aquaparque-stcruz.webnode.pt; June–Nov daily 10am–6pm; charge), with a series of slides, flumes, wave pools and other watery delights.

The main road along the coast towards Funchal passes **Caniço 20**, a village of two halves. Uphill is the original village, built around an imposing 18th-century church, with the pink-walled Quinta Splendida hotel just to the south offering the chance to explore its fine 'botanical' garden.

Porto Santo's idyllic beach

Downhill, the new Caniço de Baixo is a pretty garden suburb full of holiday villas and hotels set in lush vegetation, with a steep path down to a tiny beach.

Roughly 2km (1 mile) further on, **Ponta do Garajau** is a holiday development, popular with German visitors. The road ends at a fine *miradouro*, where a statue of Christ stands with arms outstretched. There is also a splendid view west to the Bay of Funchal.

The road dropping down into Funchal winds past some of the town's smartest villas. The first landmark is the church of São Gonçalo in the parish of the same name; photographers love this spot for its classic views down to Funchal harbour. Also in the vicinity is a tiny, atmospheric chapel, which is dedicated to Nossa Senhora das Neves (Our Lady of the Snows).

PORTO SANTO

The island of Porto Santo, 40km (25 miles) northeast of Madeira, is the only other inhabited island in the archipelago, with a population of some 5,000. As desert islands go, it's not exactly undiscovered – it is accessible via a two-hour ferry crossing, or a very short (15-minute) flight – but only a handful of foreign visitors find these shores. Porto Santo is still, at heart, the resort of Madeirans, who seek what they have not: sand.

Porto Santo's prize is a 10km (6 mile) stretch of golden beach, but that's not all that distinguishes Porto Santo from Madeira. In summer the smaller island is scorched and yellow, with rust-coloured rock and cliff formations. The island is mostly quiet, apart from its three-month summer season. Out of season, even the main town seems deserted.

The frequently rough sea crossing (the return crossing is never as bad) drops passengers at Porto de Abrigo, on the eastern tip of the island. From the dock it is a short taxi or bus ride, or a 20-minute walk, to reach **Vila Baleira** ㉑ (sometimes referred to as **Porto Santo Town**), the island's only settlement of notable size.

Vila Baleira

The centre of Vila Baleira is a small, triangular plaza, comprising a little town hall and a church that has now been restored after more than three centuries of use. **Nossa Senhora da Piedade** (Our Lady of Piety) was originally founded just after the island's discovery in the early to mid-15th century. The present church was rebuilt after pirates destroyed the original in 1667, though part of it, the Morgada chapel, did survive.

Porto Santo's claim to fame, beyond its sandy beach, is its connection with Christopher Columbus. The town's major attraction is a house, built from rough-hewn stone, that stands next to the church, set back a

Nossa Senhora da Piedade, Vila Baleira

little off the square: the **Casa Museu Cristóvão Colombo** (House-Museum of Christopher Columbus; Tue–Fri 10am–12.30pm, 2–5.30pm, July–Sept to 7pm and also Sun 10am–1pm; charge) dates from the 15th century.

The story of Columbus and the Madeiran archipelago is not entirely apocryphal, unlike so many other tales related to the islands. Columbus did marry Felipa Moniz Perestrelo, the granddaughter of the first governor of Porto Santo, Bartolomeu Perestrelo, but there is no strong evidence that this building was ever his home. That does not stop the museum claiming that Columbus lived here from 1478 to 1480 and that his tragically short-lived son, Diego, was born a *Portosantense* in this house.

Regardless of the truth, Casa Musei Cristóvão Colombo is worth a visit. Displays include period pieces, memorabilia, replicas, maps, paintings and sketches, but no personal effects or anything directly linked to the man himself. Another curious enigma about Columbus that has baffled historians is that no reliable likeness of him has ever survived. Take a look at the many different and imaginary portraits in the museum and then compare them with the dashing, modern bust of him in the public gardens by the quay.

Sleepy feral cats, Porto Santo

The liveliest street in Vila Baleira is Rua João Gonçalves Zarco, situated on the other side of the river from the plaza, running down to the sea. The street is home to the town's small market and a number of old shops and bars, full of character. The main square is Largo

Portela's windmills

do Pelourinho (Pillory Square), where, as the name indicates, local offenders were once punished.

An Island Tour

Porto Santo is absolutely tiny – less than 11km (6 miles) by 6km (4 miles). It does not require much sightseeing, which is good, because most people just come to bake on the beach. Hiring a car is expensive, and what there is to see is usually near the main roads.

Taxis will take you around the island, giving their own tours at fixed prices (see page 128). Pick up a leaflet from the tourist office and ask for a driver who can speak your language.

Heading around the island in a counter-clockwise direction, the first stop is the lookout point of **Portela** (163m/535ft). From here, you can survey the whole 9km (6 miles) of the golden, sandy beach. Head north, however, and the desolate nature of the landscape is inescapable. Crop yields are poor, partly because of the chronic lack of water, and fields that were once tended are now deserted. For most people, earning a living from tourism is more appealing than toiling in the fields.

The island's highest peak, at 517m (1,695ft), is **Pico do Facho 22**, situated around 1.5km (1 mile) due north of Portela. You will need to don hiking boots to get to the summit. Its name, which means Peak of the Torch, derives from the warning beacons that were lit here in the days when French and Algerian pirates posed a threat to the island.

The circular road now arcs north to the diminutive village of **Camacha**, where the Museu Cardina (Wed 10.30am–6.30pm, Thu–Sun 10.30am–12.30pm & 2.30–4.30pm) centres on a picturesque old windmill and has models and tools illustrating the area's past. Nearby, a ramshackle winery with an antique wooden press produces the local Porto Santo wine. If it is closed, you can still sample the wine in one of the village's several restaurant-bars.

A minor road heads west out of Camacha to **Fonte da Areia** (Sand Spring), where the rugged coastline is particularly lovely. Sandstone cliffs and rocks have been weathered into interesting

False Prophets, Magical Sands

The inhabitants of Porto Santo are sometimes referred to by Madeirans as *profetas* (prophets) – the result of a strange episode in the 16th century, when a local shepherd started a religious cult. Not only did he claim to be able to predict the future, he held people in sway by stating he had the power to list their most intimate secrets and sins. Fortunately, the cult was short-lived, and the *Portosantenses* resumed normality.

Magical powers of a different kind are attributed to the island's beach, which is said to hold curative properties that alleviate all kinds of aches and pains. Many Madeirans are convinced of its benefits and bury themselves up to their necks in sand.

shapes and small caves. A spring filtering through the rocks is the source of the island's mineral water, said to guarantee eternal youth.

The main road continues its loop, almost bringing you back to Vila Baleira, before a minor road heads north again towards **Pico do Castelo**. It is only a couple of hundred metres/yards from Pico do Facho, and from its height of 437m (1,433ft), accessible by

Exploring Calhau da Serra on a quad bike

car, it provides a commanding view itself.

The old, rusted cannons are all that remain of the fortifications that once protected the islanders from pirates – it is a popular spot for picnics and barbecues. Porto Santo's airfield, which was much larger than the one in Madeira before the latter was expanded, lies just below; beyond it is the vivid green of Porto Santo's golf course, contrasting with the tawny hues of the rest of the island.

A favourite picnic spot is **Morenos**, located towards the southwest tip of the island, although it is close to, and looking out over, the north coast. It is neat and well-tended with sunshades, flowers and seats, and enjoys a picturesque view over to the tiny **Ilhéu de Ferro** (Isle of Iron). The last viewpoint of the tour is **Pico das Flores**, at 184m (603ft).

Directly beneath Pico das Flores is the southern end of the beach and Porto Santo's southwest tip, known as **Ponta da Calheta**. The rest of the island's beach is an uninterrupted expanse, backed by attractive but slightly featureless dunes. Here, however, there are small bays with rocky outcrops and you can enjoy a beautiful view across to the Ilheu de Baixo.

WHAT TO DO

SHOPPING

Madeira is an outstanding shopping destination, given its long craft heritage. The island is renowned for wicker items, exquisite handmade lace and embroidery, gorgeous flowers and local wines. Traditional, labour-intensive methods and quality are still respected in Madeira. Unlike the Canary Islands, Madeira offers no tax concessions for visiting shoppers, so this is not the place to come in search of cheap electrical items, designer clothes, cameras or watches.

Best Buys

Wicker

You will find an outstanding array of wicker items – everything from linen-, shopping- and picnic-baskets to tables, chairs and trays. While many items are attractive and inexpensive, the impracticality of taking them home – especially as wicker is not expensive in most parts of the world – might suggest opting for more convenient souvenirs. Accustomed to exporting, though, most companies will gladly send large items to Europe and North America for you. The Relógio (Clock Tower) wicker centre in Camacha (see page 45) allows you to watch wickerwork in the making. It is far more interesting than it sounds: items are skilfully crafted using both hands and feet, and occasionally even the teeth as well.

Midday breaks

Madeirans do not take a midday siesta, but most businesses, including shops, close for a one- or two-hour lunch break.

Carnaval celebrations in Funchal

Needlework

Madeira's hand embroidery is unsurpassed. This disappearing art form – still going strong in Madeira – is an amalgam of styles and techniques that has evolved over more than 150 years. Along with fortified wine, embroidery and lacemaking are Madeira's superlative exports, and in Funchal you have ample opportunity to visit factories or workshops where the final touches are put to these painstakingly produced items. However, you are unlikely to see much actual manufacture, as the vast majority of the work is done at home by local women (some estimate that more than 10,000 are involved in the industry). Madeira creates and exports table linens, sheets, dresses, blouses, handkerchiefs and even wedding dresses of extraordinary delicacy. Tapestries range from copies of Old Master paintings to traditional pastoral scenes.

If you are used to machine-made, mass-produced embroidered items, you may be in for price-tag shock: a full set of meticulously detailed table linens can take up to two years to make, so they aren't cheap (although, measured as a reflection of someone's income for that length of time, they are). If you value the time, effort and craft that goes into these items, the price is likely to seem reasonable.

Handmade embroidery

To be sure that any needlework item is genuine (as opposed to an inferior import or machine-made piece), look for a lead seal (or more often these days a hologram) with an 'M', the emblem of IBTAM. This seal confirms the piece has been certified by the **Instituto de Bordado, Tapeçaras e Artesanato da Madeira**

Traditional knitwear for sale

(Institute of Madeiran Embroidery, Tapestry and Handicrafts), an official island organisation that has a museum on Rua Visconde de Anadia 44 (Mon–Fri 10am–12.30pm, 2– 5.30pm). There you will find a tapestry known as the *Allegory of Madeira*, which employed 14 young women over a period of three years and contains an estimated 7 million stitches.

Other Handicrafts

Though wicker and needlework are the biggest sellers, other craft items also make good souvenirs and gifts. **Boots** made from soft goatskin are part of the national costume (women's versions have red leather trim around the ankle). The boot and leather goods seller just outside the entrance of Funchal's Mercado dos Lavradores is worth a visit. The boots worn by the *carreiros*, the sled-men who push the Monte toboggans, are also available (as are the **straw hats**, old-style boaters, that they wear).

Bring a bird of paradise home

Ceramics and pottery are some of the most popular items on sale throughout Portugal. Most of the items you will find in Madeira, such as pretty hand-painted plates, planters, jugs and jars, come from the mainland – but if you are not visiting other parts of Portugal, Madeira is a good place to pick them up at bargain prices.

Other items include **marquetry**, a recently revived island craft that is featured on small boxes, pictures and furniture. The **brinquinho** is Madeira's answer to the tambourine, in which miniature cymbals are clashed together by costumed dolls 'dancing' round a maypole. You will find thick **knitwear** – pullovers, hats and gloves – at many shops up in the mountains. Unexpectedly chilly weather might make these a good impulse buy. Many of these wintry items are imported from the north of Portugal.

Food and Drink

Madeira cake and wine are extremely long-lasting, so you can safely bring some back home. Genuine Madeira cake, *bolo de mel* (honey cake), sold in many different sizes, is very different from what you get at home; it is a delicious, dark, heavy cake, similar to gingerbread. Despite its name, it is made from molasses, not honey. It lasts for up to a year and goes very well with a dry Madeira wine. You will also find plentiful supplies of traditional biscuits, honey, jams and marmalades.

Most visitors take home a bottle or two of Madeira wine (see page 99). Connoisseurs with money to burn hunt down vintage bottles – you can still turn up rare bottles like a 1795 Barbeito Terrantez or 1900 Malavasia Solera (Henriques & Henriques).

Other alcoholic drinks that you might want to take home include *branquinha* (*aguardente* with a stick of sugar cane in the bottle), or a local liqueur such as *licor de maracujá* (passionfruit) or *ginja* (cherry liqueur).

Collectables

Madeira is not noted for antiques, but stamps, coins, banknotes and vintage postcards are of interest to many collectors. A shop specialising in these items is at Avenida Arriaga 75 (Marina Shopping Centre, Shop C; tel: 291-223 070).

Flowers

Recreating a lush Madeiran garden isn't easy, but you can still take home souvenir flamingo flowers (*anthuriums*), orchids and bird of paradise flowers (*strelitzias*, or *estrelícias* in Portuguese). The latter in particular will last quite a while after your return home. Most shops will box these for storage in the aircraft hold and deliver them either to your hotel or the airport on the day you leave. Orchid plants and flowers can be bought from Jardim Orquídea, Shop 202, in the Marina Shopping Centre on Avenida Arriaga 75.

Where to Shop

Funchal's central area contains the best variety of shops and local products on the island. The main shopping streets are Fernão Ornelas, Ferreiros, Queimada de Cima and Queimada de Baixo, which together make up the city centre. The vast majority

Brightly costumed flower seller in Funchal's market

of Funchal's shops are small and independently owned.

For the best possible introduction to all of the island's handicrafts and saleable products, visit the **Casa do Turista** (Rua do Conselheiro and José Silvestre Ribeiro 2; tel: 291-224 907) on the seafront. The first few rooms are carefully laid out with pieces of antique shelving displaying fragile breakable items; beyond them, you will find a fairly conventional department store that stocks Portuguese ceramics, porcelain, wines, embroidery, dolls and inexpensive souvenirs. Out the back on the terrace is a 'mini-village', where a little *palheiro* (see page 60), a house with a weaving loom and an old-fashioned shop, re-create a bit of old Madeira.

Competing with Casa do Turista is the indoor handicraft and tourist market at **Eira do Serrado**. It sells excellent lace and embroidered items, leather goods, and a great selection of vintage Madeiran wine, with bottles dating back to the 19th century (for a hefty price, of course). Next door is the Estalagem Eira do Serrado, a hotel and restaurant with stunning mountain views.

For needlework, visit any of Funchal's factories, which put the finishing touches on items and act principally as showrooms, selling direct to the public. The biggest is **Patrício & Gouveia Sucessores** (Rua do Visconde de Anadia 34; tel: 291-220 801); it offers weekday tours. Keep an eye out for other outlets marked by small signs in doorways, including **Bazar**

Oliveiras (Rua das Murcas 6; tel: 291-224 632) and **Madeira Supérbia** (Rua do Carmo 27; tel: 291-224 023).

While virtually every tourist shop displays wicker items, **Café Relógio** (Largo da Achada, Camacha; tel: 291-922 114) wins for sheer volume. It is Madeira's 'All Things Wicker', with items ranging from the most conventional to the most implausible.

There are flower sellers along Avenida Arriaga near the Sé (Cathedral) as well as inside the **Mercado dos Lavradores**. A shop specialising in selling and packaging flowers for long-distance transport is **Casa das Flores A Rosa** (Rua Imperatriz Dona Amélia 126; tel: 291-764 111). The shop suggests that customers order flowers three days before departure.

For Madeira wines, the most atmospheric place to shop is the **Adegas de São Francisco** (see page 29), in Avenida Arriaga next to the tourist office. It has tasting rooms where you can even taste vintage wines dating from 1920, a shop selling the three brands now owned by the Madeira Wine Company (Blandy, Cossart Gordon and Leacock), and a book and souvenir shop. Other possibilities for wine in Funchal

Colourful Characters

Madeiran street flower sellers wear traditional costume – not only good for business, but required by law. Ladies in cheerful garb, as colourful as the flowers they hawk, gather alongside the cathedral at the main city market.

Younger girls wear the same red and yellow striped skirts, often with a red bolero jacket and red cape, for folk-dance demonstrations. Men wear white linen trousers and white shirts, with red cummerbunds. Black skullcaps, with curly tassels like candle wicks, are worn by both men and women, as are the native *botachãs* (literally, plain boots), made from tanned ox hide and goat skin. Women's boots are distinguished by a red band (see page 75).

include **Diogos Loja de Bebidas** (Avenida Arriaga 48; tel: 291-233 357) and the **Garrafeira do Mercado Wine Shop** (in the Mercado dos Lavradores). The winery and shop of **Henriques & Henriques Vinhos**, producers of award-winning wines, is located in Câmara de Lobos (Estrada Santa Clara 10; tel: 291-941 551).

If you have run out of things to read by the pool, check out **Julber** (Marina Shopping Centre, Shop 238, Avenida Arriaga 75) or the old-fashioned **Livraria Esperança** (Rua dos Ferreiros 119; tel: 291-221 116).

ENTERTAINMENT

Madeira does not rank with the Balearic or Canary Islands in terms of lively, night-time entertainment; it's much more of a low-key place than that. Although Funchal has a few pubs, bars, discos and even a well-attended casino with revues, the majority of visitors do not come to the island in search of a hedonistic nightlife.

The nucleus of the tourist nightlife scene consists mainly of the major hotels and their bars and nightclubs. At Funchal's **Casino da Madeira** (Avenida do Infante; tel: 291-231 121), in the grounds of the Pestana Casino Park hotel, you can play blackjack and roulette, and take a turn at the slot machines. An admission fee is charged, which covers a free drink and some gambling chips. You will need to take your passport if you wish to do more than hit the ground-level slot machines; the real gambling is upstairs. The casino is open Sun–Thur 3pm–3am, Fr–Sat 4pm–4am.

Nightlife

If gambling isn't your scene, the casino entertainment complex goes for the *tropicalia* quotient with its **Copacabana Bar** (tel: 291-231 121), which has dinner shows Wednesday

Fireworks over Funchal's harbour during the Atlantic Festival

to Saturday and dancing to live bands and DJs every night. The other principal hotel for nightlife is the Pestana Carlton Madeira (see page 135), which puts on similar themed evenings, plus classical concerts and children's shows.

Young people head for the Café do Teatro (Avenida Arriaga, next to the municipal theatre; tel: 291-249 959), Dó Fá Sol (Largo das Fontes; tel: 291-241 464) and O Molhe on top of the fortress in the cruise-ship harbour (Estrada da Pontinha; Fri–Sat midnight–6am; tel: 291-203 840). Rua Imperatriz Dona Amélia (behind the Savoy Hotel) has a number of restaurants and bars, including Prince Albert, an English pub (tel: 291-235 793), and Gloria Latina (Rua Imperatriz Dona Amélia 101; tel: 291-225 182), which has live music. Nearby, O Fugitivo (Rua Imperatriz Dona Amélia 68; tel: 291-222 003) is a popular nightclub with Brazilian dancers and transvestite shows six nights a week (Mon–Sat 10pm–6am with shows at midnight, 1.30am and 3.30am).

Dancers during the Blessed
Sacrament Festival of Santa Cruz

Vespas Discoteca (Avenida Francisco Sá Carneiro, opposite the container port; tel: 291-234 800; Wed, Fri, Sat midnight–6am) has a laser show and attracts lots of young people in serious party mood.

For more down-to-earth nightlife, two places offer regular *fado* evenings. These are **Arsénio's** restaurant (Rua de Santa Maria 169; tel: 291-224 007) and **Marcelino Pão e Vinho** (Travessa das Torres 22; 10pm–2am; tel: 291-220 216), a wine bar located to the north of the Zona Velha. Wailing *Fado* songs, accompanied by classical guitar, generally deal with the hardships of love and life. Folk-dancing evenings are a regular feature at hotels; and one popular tour is to the **Café Relógio** in the wicker-weaving town of Camacha (see pages 45), where the dancers are reputed to be Madeira's very best.

Funchal's **Teatro Municipal** is the only place that regularly stages theatrical entertainment. It is worth a visit, if only to see the theatre itself. Dating from 1888, it has recently been restored to its original splendour, and produces most of the performing arts. It is the centrepiece of the annual **Atlantic Festival**, held here in June. This festival attracts some of the big names in the classical music world, and the best of the concerts are broadcast on the island's radio station.

Throughout the year, students and teachers from the local conservatoire perform at atmospheric venues such as the Quinta das Cruzes museum (see page 34). These concerts are advertised in the window of Funchal's tourist information centre on Avenida Arriaga.

FESTIVALS

Madeira has four major festivals: Carnival, Flower Festival, Wine Festival and New Year's Eve. As long as you don't mind the crowds, these can be the best time to visit the island.

Carnival

Staged in February (occasionally in March), the pre-Lenten **Carnaval** (Carnival) is celebrated in the streets of Funchal with Brazilian-style samba rhythms. However, don't expect the hedonism or sensuality of the celebrations in Rio, Salvador or Tenerife – Funchal is too restrained for that.

Dance Roots

Many of Madeira's music and dance traditions date back to the island's colonisation. They evoke rural and courtship rituals, as well as less happy moments in the island's history. Dances reflect the importance of labour; jaunty jigs mimic the crushing of grapes with bare feet (a practice much rarer now than it once was) and slower numbers act out the carrying of heavy baskets.

The happy rhythm of these dances contrasts with the overtly sombre *Dance of the Ponta do Sol*, which harks back to Ponta do Sol's days as slave quarters. The steps are short; the feet, as if chained, hardly lifted off the ground; and the head is submissively bowed (slaves were forbidden to look their masters in the eye).

Two musical instruments played are uniquely Madeiran: the *machête*, a guitar-like instrument plucked to a rather monotonous beat, and the extraordinary *brinquinho*, a percussion instrument that features tiny folk-dancing dolls holding bells and castanets.

Flower Festival

The **Festa da Flor** in late April or early May is a crowd-pleaser. It includes floats – decorated in beautiful, inventive floral creations – parading through Funchal's streets. Two events peripheral to the main parade should not be missed. One is the **children's parade**, in which each child carries a single flower and places it in a hole in a 'Wall of Hope' in the Praça do Município. Covered in flowers, the wall is a moving sight. Once the parade is finished, an **exhibition** of the award-winning displays is staged in a lovely old house in Rua dos Castanheiros.

Wine Festival

Festivals take place in wine villages, such as Estreito de Câmara de Lobos, to celebrate the September harvest. You may occasionally see grapes being crushed the traditional

Funchal's Flower Festival

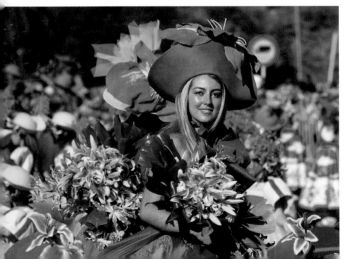

way: barefoot men and women treading the grapes; this practice was widespread on the island until fairly recently. Wine samples are also served from traditional goatskin bags once used to store and carry wine.

New Year's Eve

Madeira's biggest and most spectacular festival has an international reputation. Every year, Funchal's hotels are packed, and if you want to stay on the island over New Year you will need to book accommodation many months in advance and pay a hefty premium. Many winter cruise ships anchor in Funchal harbour on 31 December to participate in the party. At midnight, all the houses in town switch on all their lights, opening all the doors and windows, setting the hillside ablaze with light. The cruise ships crank up their floodlights, and the parties begin. As the New Year rings in, a splendid fireworks display erupts.

Religious Festivals

Several **religious festivals** also take place throughout the year, but one especially stands out – the **Feast of the Assumption**, known more parochially as the Festival of Nossa Senhora do Monte (Our Lady of Monte), is celebrated on 15 August in Monte. Pilgrims flock from all around the island to kiss the image of the patron saint, and some ascend the final 68 steps to the church on their knees.

To the many Madeirans who believe that the Lady of Monte has carried them through troubled times, the pilgrimage is an obligation. For these people the Monte church is akin to Lourdes. The sick and infirm arrive in droves in search of miraculous cures. Once the pious devotions are over, wine flows, fireworks explode and *espetada* (kebab) stalls flourish, before Monte returns to normality for another 364 days.

SPORTS

With no beaches to speak of, and scarcely enough flat ground for a playing surface, Madeira may not be the first destination that springs to mind for a sporting holiday. However, there are sufficient opportunities for most active holiday-makers and excellent ones for those who enjoy walking and hiking.

Spectator Sports

The only sport to watch on Madeira is **football**. Islanders are wild about *futebol*, and two of the island's teams – Marítimo and Nacional,

The footpaths alongside *levadas* make great walking trails

play in the first division of the Portuguese league. Marítimo's stadium is on Rua Dr Pita, while Nacional's is high above Funchal at Choupana. See the local newspaper for fixtures or ask your hotel concierge.

Walking & Hiking

Mountainous Madeira, with its network of *levada* trails (see page 59), is perfect for walkers of all ages and abilities. Such watercourses exist elsewhere, but nowhere are they so accessible nor do they cover such a great area. The island's irrigation system is composed of some 2,100km (1,300 miles) of channels. The paths that run alongside them are mostly gentle but exhilarating at the same time. More serious trekkers, with cross-country or mountain walking on their minds, can choose from one of the walks listed below:

Boca da Corrida–Encumeada (moderate; 5 hours): views of Curral das Freiras and Ribeiro do Poco valley. **Pico do Arieiro–Pico Ruivo–Achada do Teixeira** (moderate–difficult; 4 hours): a trip to Madeira's highest peak. **Ponta de São Lourenço** (moderate; 4 hours): great rock formations, flora and views of the Atlantic. **The Caniçal tunnel–Boca do Risca–Larano** (easy; 3.5 hours): a walk along the north coast between Boca do Risco and Porto da Cruz; terrific flora and sea views.

All these can be undertaken alone by experienced walkers or with local guides (see page 119), but it is best to know in advance what you are likely to encounter and a reliable walkers' guidebook (see page 124) is a good investment.

Golf

This is a year-round sport in Madeira. The island has 45 holes of championship golf divided between two courses, both of which are esteemed for their scenic beauty. Every spring the Madeira Island Open, part of the pga European Tour, takes place at Santo da Serra Golf Club. The 27-hole **Clube de Golf Santo da Serra** (tel: 291-550 100; www.santodaserragolf.com) is one of Europe's most exciting courses, suitable for all levels. Designed by Robert Trent Jones, the course is close to the picturesque village of Santo da Serra, east of Funchal, and has stupendous views to the sea below. The **Palheiro Golf Club** (tel: 291-790 120, www. palheirogolf.com) is in the

> ### Advice for hikers
>
> If you are going to do some of Madeira's serious walking trails, take warm clothing, as the weather can change very abruptly. Hiking boots with good support and traction are a good idea to combat uneven or loose surfaces, and sunblock is essential.

A lido complex in Porto da Cruz

São Gonçalo hills, 15 minutes east of the centre of Funchal. The course, designed by Cabel Robinson, has 18 holes and is set in the Quinta do Palheiro Ferreiro gardens. So spectacular are the views over the bay and city that it is a great place to visit, even if you don't play golf. On Porto Santo, the **Porto Santo Golfe** (tel: 291-983 778) is an 18-hole course designed by Seve Ballesteros and located in a green valley on the slopes of the Pico Ana Ferreira mountain, with sea breezes and coastal scenery.

Tennis

Flat land is at such a premium in Funchal that even the likes of Reid's and the Royal Savoy can only afford two tennis courts each. If your hotel does not have its own court, try **Quinta do Magnólia Park** (tel: 291-764 598), where the facilities are excellent (including floodlights) and inexpensive. The park also has squash courts and an exercise trail.

Horse Riding

Lessons and cross-country riding are offered by the **Club Ipismo** (Quinta Vale Pires, Caminho dos Pretos, São João Latrão; tel: 291-792 582), just outside Funchal. Horses can also be hired from the **Riding Club of Choupana** at Hotel Estrelícia (tel: 291-792 582) and the **Quinta do Pântano** (Casais Próximos, Santo da Serra; tel: 291-552 577) and on the island of Porto Santo from the **Centro Hípico** (tel: 291-983 258).

Swimming

Although much of Madeira's coast drops dizzily into the sea, offering little or no safe access for bathers, there is an artificial beach at Calheta, and a number of **lido complexes** around the coast offering swimming pools and cafés, along with concrete jetties that lead out to safe sea bathing and diving areas. Among the best are the lidos at Seixal, Ponta Delgada and Porto da Cruz. For something more natural, there is the small black-sand beach at Prainha and the bathing complex east of São Jorge, combining a swimming pool with sea bathing and a river pool created in the bend of the São Jorge estuary. You can have a dip in the semi-natural pools at **Porto Moniz** on the island's extreme northwest tip, or enjoy slides and flumes at Santa Cruz's **Aquaparque** (see page 65).

Beach lovers should hop islands to the 9km (6 miles) of sands of **Porto Santo** (though sunshine is only really guaranteed June to August). You can fly with tap/Air Portugal (15-minute flight) or take the ferry, which leaves daily at 8am (tel: 291-210 300; www.portosantoline.pt).

Most of the good hotels have swimming pools and there is year-round swimming pool open to the public at the **Complexo Balnear do Lido** (Lido Complex; tel: 291-762 217) in Funchal's Tourist Zone. There are two main pools, plus a children's pool, sunbathing along the terraces and rocks

Diving is popular on Madeira

by the sea, and good catering facilities. What's more, it's cheap. The only drawback is large crowds in summer. Other good inexpensive public pools are in the **Quinta do Magnólia** park (Rua Dr Pita) or the **Clube Naval**, along the seafront promenade in Funchal's hotel zone. Some larger hotels, such as the Royal Savoy, may allow non-residents into their pools, but at a price guaranteed to exclude local people.

Diving

Divers are in luck in Madeira, since one of Europe's first underwater nature reserves was created along the Garajau coastline. Besides abundant, colourful fish, divers can see shipwrecks. Sea temperatures vary between 18° and 24°C (64–75°F). Several diving schools are recommended. **Tubarão Madeira** (tel: 291-794 124; www.scuba-madeira. com), in the Pestana Palms hotel on Praia Formosa, 3km (2 miles) west of Funchal, offers wreck-, night-, cave- and Nitrox-diving. **Madeira Oceanos**, based at the Dom Pedro Baia hotel in Machico (tel: 291-776 531; www.madeiraoceanos. com), offers everything from beginners' courses and single dives to advanced tuition. Alternatively the **Atalaia Diving Club** at the Royal Orchid Hotel in Caniço (tel: 291-934 330; www.atalaia-madeira.com), offers diving equipment for hire, and various courses. A single dive costs around €30, while a novice diving course, including equipment hire, will run to €250 or more.

Big Game Fishing and Boat Trips

In the deep Atlantic, just beyond Madeira's shallow waters, you can catch – according to the season – giant blue marlin, bonito, tuna (big-eye, blue-fin and yellow-fin), barracuda, swordfish, wahoo and shark (hammerhead, maco and blue). Madeira's sport-fishing companies operate a 'tag and release' scheme whereby any fish caught are returned unharmed to the wild after photographing.

The very best deep-sea fishing is from June to September. **Turipesca** (tel: 291-231 063) charters set out from Funchal Marina. Captain Peter Bristow of **Fish Madeira** (Travessa das Virtudes, São Martinho 23, 9000–163 Funchal; tel: 291-752 685; www.fishmadeira.com) also runs big-game fishing expeditions. Big-game fishing expeditions generally cost upwards of €125 per person per day.

Funchal Marina where deep-sea fishing boats can be hired

CHILDREN'S MADEIRA

Madeira has several attractions aimed at families, including the **Madeira Story Centre** in Funchal (see page 36), with computers and interactive games based on Madeira's history. The **Madeira Theme Park** in Santana (see page 60) has adventure playgrounds and a boating lake; the **Aquarium and Science Centre** in Porto Moniz and the **Caves and Vulcanology Centre** in São Vicente (see page 53) are also likely to appeal. Given all these choices, most children should find a visit to the island an enjoyable experience, especially if it coincides with any of the major festivals (see page 83 and Calendar of Events, page 93). The festivals with greatest appeal for children are the famous **Flower Festival**, with the children's parade and 'Wall of Hope', and **Carnaval**. When all else fails, the swimming pools (see page 89) are enough to satisfy almost any child.

If you don't want to hire a car, both the **Jardim Botânico** (see page 38), with its bird park, and the **Palheiro Gardens** (see page 40) are accessible by bus. The park on the hill of **Monte** makes an excellent playground, with the added thrill of ascending or descending by cable car (see page 41).

Children will enjoy a cable-car ride

Activities for slightly older children include horse riding and *levada* walks. A very enjoyable nature day – identifying plants and flowers, dipping toes into the refreshing irrigation canals, cooling off in tunnels, picnicking on a hillside – can be had at any of the *levada* paths highlighted in this book.

Calendar of Events

Madeirans celebrate many festivals throughout the year, some primarily organised for tourists, others deeply rooted in religion and folklore. Many of the celebrations are the feast days of saints.

6 January *Festa dos Reis*: Funchal and elsewhere. Three Kings Festival and close of Christmas festivities.

20 January *São Sebastião* celebrated in Caniçal, Câmara de Lobos.

February/March *Carnaval*: huge festival in Funchal, culminating in a colourful procession on the Saturday before Shrove Tuesday (see page 83).

Last week April/first week May *Festa da Flôr*: Funchal Flower Festival and Ceremony of the Wall of Hope (see page 84).

June *Atlantic Festival*: musical performances at weekends in Funchal's Teatro Municipal and other venues, and firework displays over the harbour.

23–24 June *São João da Ribeira* (Feast of St John) celebrated in Funchal, São João, Câmara de Lobos, Ponta do Sol and elsewhere.

29 June *São Pedro* (St Peter), patron saint of fishermen: bonfires and boat procession at Ribeira Brava, Ponta do Pargo and Câmara de Lobos.

July *Feira Agro-Pecuária*: agricultural fair and festival, Porto Moniz.

2 July 'Rediscovery of Madeira' and the first landing of Portuguese sailors in 1420, celebrated in Machico.

Late July *24 Horas a Bailar*: 24-hour folk-dance marathon, Santana.

15 August Festival of *Nossa Senhora do Monte* (Our Lady of Monte). Pilgrims flock to Monte from all around the island, some climb the steps to the church on their knees.

Early September Madeira Wine Festival: grape harvesting in Estreito de Câmara de Lobos, with shows and exhibitions here and in Funchal.

8–9 September *Festa do Senhor dos Milagres*: nocturnal procession in Machico honouring the Lord of Miracles.

September (third week) *Festa de Nossa Senhora da Piedade* in Caniçal.

1 November *Festa da Castanha*: Chestnut Festival in Curral das Freiras.

December Christmas illuminations in Funchal, exhibitions at weekends, culminating in a big party and firework display on New Year's Eve.

EATING OUT

Funchal has been catering for visitors since Victorian times. While it's not Portugal's dining capital, there are plenty of good restaurants. For international or haute cuisine, the best places are in the hotel zone, the up-market, far end of the Old Town, and the touristy marina establishments. If you would rather eat with local people, try the side streets around the cathedral, Rua Carreira or cafés along Rua Dom Carlos I.

Most Madeiran restaurants stick to traditional opening times, with lunch *(almoço)* served from around noon to 3pm and dinner *(jantar)* from 7 to 10pm. Many restaurants in Funchal offer all-day service, not closing after lunch, and you will never have any problems finding cafés serving snacks all day. For breakfast *(pequeno almoço)*, most Madeirans start their day with a sweet pastry and coffee. Hotels usually serve the standard international buffet, with bacon and egg, cold meats, cheeses, fruit and cereals.

What to Eat

Madeira has its own typical dishes, in addition to Portuguese specialities. As a rule, the food here is simple; it uses fresh ingredients and is served up in hearty portions. A Madeiran trademark is the excellent island bread, *bolo do caco*, which is made from flour and sweet potato and normally served with garlic butter *(manteiga de alho)*.

Starters. Soup is always on the menu. The best is usually Madeira's own *tomate e cebola*, a delicious soup made from tomatoes and onions, and very often served *com ovo* (with a poached egg floating on top). A Portuguese staple, *caldo verde* (literally green broth), is a thick soup

Seasoning savvy

Salt and pepper are not usually placed on the table. But you will be given them if you ask: *sal e pimenta, faz favor.*

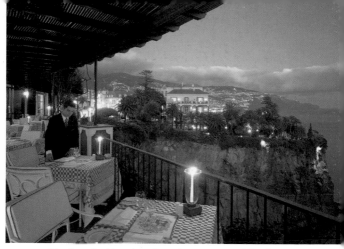
The breathtaking view from the terrace at Villa Cipriani

of potato purée with finely shredded cabbage or kale. Another soup from the mainland is *açorda*, thicker still and made with bread and garlic.

Basic fish restaurants serve *caramujos* (winkles), which look unappetising as you prise them out from their tiny shells, but taste fine, and *lapas grelhadas* (grilled limpets). The latter are a meatier version of mussels (some of them taste almost like liver) and are served grilled in the shell. At the other end of the price spectrum, look out for smoked swordfish *(espadarte fumado)*, a Portuguese delicacy that is a little like smoked salmon, but tastes less sweet and has a coarser texture.

Fish and Seafood. Madeira's speciality, seen on menus across the island, is the *espada*, a fearsome-looking, ink-black, eel-like beast, which can grow to around 1m (3ft) in length and has long, needle-sharp teeth. Despite its appearance, the nasty creature has delicious white meat. Some restaurants serve it poached, but more often fillets are fried, often with a banana, which complements the flavour surprisingly well. Note that *espada* and *espadarte* (swordfish; see page 95), though similar-sounding, are different fish.

The other island fish is tuna (*atum*), often served in steaks (*bife de atum*) and with a Madeira wine sauce (*a Madeirense*). Maize or cornmeal (*milho*) deep-fried in cubes (also an island speciality) is often served with tuna, and is offered as a standard accompaniment to many meals in *típicos* (rustic restaurants) around the island.

You will find a wide selection of other fish on the menu, usually grilled or fried, including: *pargo* and *besugo*, which are types of sea bream; *garoupa* and *cherne*, types of grouper; and *bacalhau*, the famous salt-cod, cooked in many different ways. It is often served in a casserole, which tends to hide its distinctive, preserved flavour. Try it *cozido* (boiled). Other fish are

Grilled limpets are a speciality; they taste better than they look shark, swordfish and *bodião* (parrot-fish).

Two slow-simmering Portuguese favourites that appear on restaurant menus are *caldeirada*, a rich stew made from fish, potato, tomato and onion, and *cataplana*. The latter is named after the hinged pressure cooker made of copper that is used to cook a mixture of clams, ham, sausage, onion, garlic, parsley, white wine and paprika (ingredients vary from one restaurant to the next).

Two local favourites are octopus (*polvo*), served cold in a salad or hot, fried or stewed; and squid (*lulas*), grilled, fried or stuffed (*recheado*). Shellfish do not flourish in Madeiran waters, and all prawns and lobsters are imported.

A menu that quotes a price – usually for shellfish or fresh fish – as '*preço V*' means variable, or market, price. Ascertain the day's market price before ordering.

Meat. *Espetada* (not to be confused with *espada* or *espadarte*) is the typical Madeiran meat dish, a kebab of beef traditionally threaded on a skewer of sweet bay. In many restaurants, however, it is served on a metal skewer with a hook on one end, which is hung vertically from a special stand fixed to the end of your dining table. The beef is first grilled over embers of fragrant sweet bay, having been marinated in garlic and wine to make it tender and tasty – though it can occasionally still be tough. For something easier on the jaw, try pork in wine and garlic (*porco de vinho e alho*), which is marinated, tenderised and then grilled. Chicken (*frango*) is always on the menu, and may be served plain, grilled, African-style (as in *piri-piri* when it's basted in a sauce of hot chilli peppers, then grilled) or in

The fearsome-looking *espadas*

a Goan-inspired curry sauce. Ox tongue (*lingua*) served with Madeira wine sauce is also a Portuguese speciality.

Desserts. Portugal's *flã or pudim*, a type of crème caramel, is common, as is ice cream (*gelado*). A good restaurant will offer seasonal fruit after your meal, but you may have to ask for it. The island has an excellent range of exotic fruits, so sample them fresh from the market if not in a restaurant. A favourite is *anonas* or custard apple (originally from Peru). Split in half, the flesh is soft and white, with large black pips. To some, it tastes like its name, while others liken it rather more fancifully to strawberries and cream. A speciality of several tourist restaurants is fruit flambé.

Table Wines

There are various varieties of Madeiran table wine, of which Atlantis Rosé is the most famous, sold across the island. Most good restaurants stock a full complement of Portuguese wines (top restaurants will also offer foreign labels), many of which are excellent.

Portuguese wines are quite good across the board, and several regions produce truly excellent wines. You need do nothing more than tell the waiter *tinto* (red) or *branco* (white), and you can't go wrong. However, several of the best wine-producing regions have names whose use is controlled by law (*região demarcada*), and it's worth seeking out wines from the best regions. Dão and Douro in the north of Portugal produce vigorous reds and flavourful whites. Wines from the Alentejo region are also highly regarded.

Vinho Verde (literally green wine), popular all over Portugal, is named for its youth, rather than its colour, and has a slight fizz. It goes well with simple fish and seafood dishes.

The two most celebrated Portuguese wines, port and Madeira, are primarily known as dessert wines, but they may also be sipped as aperitifs. The before-dinner varieties are dry or extra dry white port, and the dry Madeiras (Sercial, Terrantez and Verdelho). These should be served slightly chilled. After dinner, sip one of the famous ruby or tawny ports (aged tawnys are especially good) or a Madeira dessert wine (Bual and Malvasia, or Malmsey).

Madeira Wine

The history of the island's eponymous drink, famous the world over, is as full and well-rounded as a bottle of the best vintage Malvasia. When the island was first settled during the 15th century, Prince Henry ordered Zarco to plant vines, brought to the island from Crete. Although wine was not planned as a major export, it became one of the most important products of the island, thanks to a combination of its notable quality and Madeira's position on the shipping lanes to the East and West Indies. The island was an obvious stopping point, where water, fresh food and wine could be taken on-board. With the rise of the British colonies in North America and the West Indies, Madeira wine was soon established as a favourite on both sides of the Atlantic, and shipped all over the British Empire.

Initially, Madeira was not a fortified wine, but gradually the addition of grape brandy became common practice in order to stabilise it on long sea voyages. During the 18th century, it was discovered that shipping the wine actually improved its longevity as well as its flavour. Producers realised that tropical heat was the key ingredient, and towards the end of the century, pipes of Madeira were loaded as ballast on transatlantic journeys in order to 'cook' them as much as possible. When it became impractical to send barrels on return trips, conditions for heating the wine had to be reproduced at home. The easiest way was simply to store barrels in lofts that soaked up abundant sunlight. Subsequently, special tanks called *estufas*, centrally heated by hot-water pipes, were employed; this system is still in use today for cheaper Madeira wines, subjecting the wine to a temperature of 35°C (95°F) for six months.

Oxidisation during the heating process renders the wine virtually indestructible. A bottle of Madeira can be kept uncorked for many months without suffering any deterioration, even when other types of fortified wine (such as port) would moulder quickly under such conditions. For this reason, there are Madeira wines from the early 1800s that are entirely drinkable today.

Choosing a Bottle. There are several types of Madeira, each named after the grape that gives that style of wine its distinctive flavour and characteristics. The lightest and driest is Sercial, which has a full-bodied, nutty flavour, not unlike an *amontillado* sherry. It is best served chilled as an aperitif. Verdelho and Terrantez are both classified as medium-dry and should be served slightly chilled. A tangy aperitif, they are also recommended as an accompaniment to soup. Bual, probably introduced by the Jesuits in the 17th century, is a rich

Madeiras of various vintages at the Adegas de São Francisco

and port-like Madeira with a splendid honeyed taste and an underlying acidity, which means that it can cut through sweet desserts and is also a good accompaniment to cheese. Finally and most famously, Malvasia (also known as Malmsey) is the richest of all, and is usually served following a meal.

Some Madeira wines are made from blends of several years, and the skill and style of the blender is what gives the wines of different shippers their individual character. The youngest component of the blend gives the stated age of the wine on the label: Finest is a blend in which the youngest is at least three years old, while Reserve and Special Reserve wines are at least five and 10 years old, respectively. The best, however, are Vintage wines, bottled after ageing in oak casks for a minimum of 20 years. The longer the wine stays in the cask, the better it will be. The wine is then kept for another two years before sale.

If you really want to impress your friends back home, buy a 75ml bottle of 1875 D'Oliveira Malvasia Madeira Family

Reserve for a mere €500 or so. If your budget doesn't stretch to that, you can pick up more recent vintages for around €20.

Other Island Drinks

After Madeira, the most famous drink produced on the island is *aguardente*, a powerful sugar cane distillation, which varies in taste from virtually unpalatable firewater to smooth, aged brandy. Look for the term *velha* (old) on the label unless you have an iron constitution. Add lemon juice and honey to *aguardente* and you have *poncha*, a delicious drink that belies its ferocious base.

Other liqueurs are distilled from the island's fruit, two notable examples being a cherry brandy from Curral das Freiras called *ginja*; and *licor de maracujá*, passion fruit liqueur (don't confuse it with the soft drink, *refrigerante de maracujá*). The local Coral lager (*cerveja*) is also excellent and very welcome on a hot day.

Liquid History

It was Shakespeare who first gave Madeira wine a literary platform, when in *Henry IV* Falstaff is accused of selling his soul for a leg of chicken and a goblet of Madeira. The real Henry IV actually died before the discovery of the island, let alone the wine. In 1478, the Duke of Clarence went one better than Falstaff and actually drowned in a barrel of Malmsey. Sir Winston Churchill was once presented with a bottle of 1792 Sercial in Reid's Hotel, then delighted his guests by placing a napkin over his arm and assuming the duties of waiter.

But Madeira wine didn't win favour with just the British. It was used to toast the American Declaration of Independence, and drunk at the Inauguration of George Washington, who was said to consume a pint of Madeira at dinner daily. Benjamin Franklin and Thomas Jefferson were also Madeira connoisseurs.

TO HELP YOU ORDER

We'd like a table. **Queríamos uma mesa**.
I'd like a/an/some … **Queria** …

bread **pão**	tea **chá**
rice **arroz**	fruit **fruta**
butter **manteiga**	wine **vinho**
salad **salada**	ice cream **gelado**
coffee **um café**	meat **carne**
soup **sopa**	milk **leite**
dessert **sobremesa**	fried **frito**
sugar **açucar**	potatoes **batatas**
fish **peixe**	grilled **grelhado**

MENU READER

alho garlic	**gambas** prawns
amêijoas baby clams	**guisado** stew
ananás pineapple	**laranja** orange
arroz rice	**legumes** vegetables
atum tuna	**linguado** sole
azeitonas olives	**lulas** squid
bacalhau cod (salted)	**maçã** apple
bife (vaca) steak (beef)	**mariscos** shellfish
bolo cake	**melancia** watermelon
borrego lamb	**mexilhões** mussels
camarões shrimps	**molho** sauce
caranguejo crab	**ovo** egg
cebola onion	**pimento** pepper
chouriço spicy sausage	**porco** pork
coelho rabbit	**presunto** ham
cogumelos mushrooms	**queijo** cheese
feijões beans	**robalo** sea bass
figos figs	**uvas** grapes
frango chicken	**vitela** veal

PLACES TO EAT

We have used the following symbols to give an idea of the price for a three-course meal for one, including wine, cover and service:

€€€€ over 50 euros   **€€** 20–30 euros
€€€ 30–50 euros   **€** below 20 euros

FUNCHAL TOWN

Apolo €€€ *Rua Dr. António Joaquim Almeida 21; tel: 291-220 099*. Enjoy traditional cuisine in a relaxed atmosphere at this informal, intimate place, which claims to be the oldest restaurant in Madeira. Choose from soups, salads, fish and meat dishes; you can dine indoors or on the outdoor pavement tables.

Armazem do Sal €€€ *Rua da Alfandega 135; tel: 291-241 285*. An unusual setting in a 400-year-old salt warehouse. Look out for the coat of arms by the door as this place isn't easy to find. A dark, rustic space, with plenty of fish and Portuguese wine on the menu. Serves lunch and dinner Monday to Friday, and dinner on Saturday.

Restaurant Caravela €€€€ *Avenida das Comunidades Madeirenses 15 (3rd floor); tel: 291-225 471*. This 30-year-old city centre restaurant is popular for its panoramic ocean views as well as the Portuguese cuisine, focusing on fresh fish and shellfish. Interior dining room and a glass-enclosed terrace. Open Mon–Sat for lunch and dinner.

Restaurant do Forte €€€€ *Forte de São Tiago, 9060-250 Funchal; tel: 291-215 580*. With a fantastic setting atop Funchal's mustard-yellow, 17th-century fort, some terrace tables here have views out to sea, peeking through the battlements. The menu includes pasta, risotto, grilled fish, and dishes such as duck in citrus sauce. Open daily for lunch and dinner.

Londres €€ *Rua da Carreira tel: 291-235 329.* A local favourite, this is a simple place serving simple dishes, of which the stand out is the grilled fish. Open Mon–Sat for lunch and dinner.

Marina Terrace €€€ *Marina do Funchal; tel: 291-230 547.* At the far end of the marina, this popular choice has a wide menu, but is particularly good for fish, shellfish, and steak, which is served sizzling on a hot slab. Open daily for lunch and dinner.

Mozart €€€€ *Don Carlos I, 50, Funchal 9060-051; tel: 291- 244 239.* Sister restaurant to that in the fort, this attractive place in the old town has walls painted in snooker-green and hung with paintings, and the maître d' is dressed in 18th-century costume. Food is sophisticated and there is regular live music. Open daily for lunch and dinner.

O Tappassol €€ *62, Rua D. Carlos I, Funchal, Madeira 9050-041; tel· 291-225 023.* In a characterful old building, decked with beautiful flowers, this establishment offers excellent, good-value local cuisine, including exceptional grilled fish. There is a great view from the terrace – book ahead for an outdoor table.

Riso €€€€ *Rua de Santa Maria 274; tel: 291-280360.* This acclaimed gem provides amazing views of the ocean from its clifftop location, with alfresco dining being the best option – tables are set under a modernist white canopy. A wide choice of rice dishes from around the world, and plenty of options for vegetarians.

FUNCHAL HOTEL ZONE

Casa Velha €€€€ *Rua Imperatriz Dona Amélia 69; tel: 291-205 600.* A formal garden-like restaurant with bamboo chairs, ferns and ceiling fans, the 'Old House' has a 19th-century colonial feel. The short Madeiran and international menu is popular with nearby hotel guests. Piano bar downstairs. Open daily for lunch and dinner.

Dona Amélia €€€ *Rua Imperatriz Dona Amélia 83; tel: 291-225 784.* This chic upstairs restaurant is a good place for a romantic dinner of *espetadas* (kebabs), grilled fish, nice salads and soups. Open daily lunch and dinner.

Les Faunes €€€€ *Estrada Monumental 139 (in Reid's Palace Hotel); tel: 291-717 030.* Reid's elegant winter restaurant is something really special, the standard bearer on Madeira for creative French cuisine. The elegant dining room overlooking the harbour is the place to eat in a refined atmosphere, with piano accompaniment. In summer, Les Faunes moves out onto the hotel's open-air terrace and becomes the Brisa Mar restaurant. Open daily for dinner, except Tue and Sat, Oct–May.

Uva €€€€ *Rua dos Aranhas 27 (in the Vine Hotel); tel: 291-009 000.* This super-stylish restaurant in the boutique Vine Hotel serves up creative cuisine in a sleek, modernist setting, with huge plate-glass windows and a great terrace making the most of fantastic views. There's an extensive wine list. Open lunch and dinner daily.

Villa Cipriani €€€€ *Reid's Palace hotel, Estrada Monumental 139; tel: 291-717 171.* Don't be put off by this great Italian restaurant being part of a hotel. Dining out on the terrace admiring the sea views from the hotel's clifftop position is a delightful way to spend an evening. Dinner served daily.

FUNCHAL TOURIST ZONE

O Tokos €€€€ *Estrada Monumental 169; tel: 291-771 019.* A tiny restaurant with an eccentric chef/owner (Felipe dos Ramos), this intimate place (just 10 or so tables) does everything well, but when the chef wheels out the trolley of fresh fish, you will be hard-pressed to order anything else. Excellent desserts and a very good wine cellar. Reservations essential. Open Tue–Sun for lunch and dinner.

Il Gallo d'Oro €€€€ *Cliff Bay Hotel, Estrada Monumental 147; tel: 291-707 700.* Madeira's only Michelin-starred restaurant serves extremely sophisticated Mediterranean and Iberian cuisine under the stewardship of Chef Benoît Sinthon. Open daily for dinner.

BEYOND FUNCHAL

Casa Velha do Palheiro €€€€ *Rua da Estalagem 23–São Gonçalo–Funchal; tel: 291-790 350.* The refined dining room in the grounds of the Quinta do Palheiro is one of the island's most elegant restaurants. Exquisite international and Portuguese dishes. Daily fixed-price and à la carte menus are available alongside a gourmet seven-course tasting menu. Superb service and wine list. Open daily for dinner. Dress code is smart casual.

O Cesto €€ *Camacha; tel: 291-922 068.* This simple neighbourhood Camacha restaurant, with attached bar, is spacious and inviting, and serves good-value, home-style cooking, specialising in chicken and roasted meats. Open for lunch Fri–Tue.

Orca €€€ *Rua Engenheiro Americo, Porto Moniz, 9270-095; tel: 291-850 000.* This seaside restaurant has big windows and a terrace, both with fantastic views over the sea. The menu offers more of a seafood theme, with fresh grilled fish and shellfish dishes.

Pousada dos Vinháticos €€€ *Fajã dos Vinháticos, Serra d'Água; tel: 291-952 344.* This chalet-style inn has an excellent restaurant with panoramic views of the surrounding mountains. It serves mostly Madeiran and Portuguese specialities, but does an excellent chateaubriand for two. Nice wine list and friendly service. Downstairs bar and outdoor terrace. Open daily for lunch and dinner.

Praça do Engeno €€ *Rua da Praia, Porto da Cruz; tel: 291-560 080.* The *engeno* of this restaurant's name refers to the location on the seafront at Porta da Cruz, inside the converted engine room of a former sugar mill. Grey basalt walls lit by modern plate glass provide the setting for a leisurely meal of fresh seafood, which you can choose for yourself from a selection laid out on a bed of ice. Open daily for lunch and dinner.

Quinta do Furão €€€ *Achada do Gramacho, Santana; tel: 291-570 100.* This rustic restaurant, part of the hotel of the same name, serves some of the finest food on the entire north coast. Surrounded by orchards and a vineyard, it offers the freshest selection of local ingredients and seafood. Open daily for lunch and dinner.

Restaurante Ribeiro Frio €€ *Ribeiro Frio; tel: 291-575 898.* A cosy bar reminiscent of an English pub leads to a chalet-like dining area with a fireplace, and there's a greenery-surrounded terrace. The house speciality is grilled trout, plucked fresh from the hatchery across the road (fed by the cold river that gives the village its name). Reserve ahead during peak season, as it is the only restaurant in the village and can get very busy when the coaches turn up. Open daily for lunch.

Taberna de Sao Vicente €€€ *Estrada Regional 104, Sao Vicente, Madeira 9240-225; tel: 291-848 034.* On the outskirts of Sao Vicente, this cosy and inviting place with checked tablecloths and sunflower-yellow walls is a friendly, family-run place. The chef proffers good seafood, including limpets and octopus, plus some traditional dishes such as *espada* cooked with banana, and a choice of excellent desserts.

PORTO SANTO

Baiana €€ *Rua do Dr Nuno S. Teixeira 7, Vila Baleira; tel: 291-983 027.* This is a busy restaurant in a great location on the town square. Popular with tourists and locals alike, it serves generous portions of both seafood and meat dishes. There are tables outside where you can sit and watch the world go by.

Pé na Agua €€€ *Porto Santo beach; tel: 291-983 114.* With a brilliant location right on the beach, this casual bar and restaurant is perfect for lunch, dinner or just a drink. Tables are located inside as well as outdoors on a terrace. Fresh seafood is the speciality, with the seafood spaghetti being a favourite. Generous portions accompany attentive service from the staff. Gets very popular at weekends.

A–Z TRAVEL TIPS

A Summary of Practical Information

A

ACCOMMODATION (see also Recommended Hotels, page 133 and Camping, page 113)

The government grades hotels and hotel-apartments (*aparthotels*) in Madeira from 2 to 5 stars. Below the rating of hotel is *estalagem*, which loosely translates as 'inn'. These may be simple hotels away from the main tourist areas, or they may be extremely comfortable, individually owned inns. The categories below *estalagem* are *albergaria*, *residência* and *pensão* – usually small bed-and-breakfast hotels with basic facilities, although a handful of *estalagems* and *albergarias* are the equivalent of 5-star hotels.

Madeira is unique in also offering *quinta* accommodation. *Quintas* are gracious mansions and villas, usually set in splendid gardens, brimming with antiques and restored to provide a standard of accommodation (and prices) equivalent to a 4- or 5-star hotel. They do not offer all the sports or facilities and amenities of a top hotel, but in terms of character and personal service they are often much better. All are limited in the number of rooms, so book early. Early booking is also recommended if you want to stay on the island between Christmas and New Year's Eve (see page 85).

Travellers familiar with Portugal might arrive in Madeira looking for a *pousada*, a luxury government-owned hotel set in a building of architectural and historical character. Madeira does not have any official *pousadas*, but the Pousada dos Vinháticos on the north–south road from Ribeira Brava to São Vicente is a privately run hotel that fits the general *pousada* principal, enjoying a tranquil, scenic setting away from the main tourist areas.

I'd like a single/double room with bath/shower. **Queria um quarto simples/duplo com banho/chuveiro.**
What's the rate per night? **Qual é o preço por noite?**

AIRPORTS

Madeira's **Santa Catarina** international airport (tel: 291-520 700; www.anam.pt/madeira) is in Santa Cruz, 22km (14 miles) east of Funchal. It used to have one of the shortest passenger runways in Europe until it was enlarged in 2000. Even so, arriving is still an adventure, and occasionally, in really bad weather, flights have to be diverted to Porto Santo.

From the airport to Funchal it is about 35 minutes by taxi or an hour by bus. During rush hour, allow double the time. Visitors can either take the city bus (€2.50), with multiple stops, the airport bus (€5) or a taxi, which has posted set fares (between €20 and €30 depending on the time of day) to Funchal's tourist or hotel zone, or city centre. Several car hire agencies have desks at the airport, and there is a small tourist information kiosk, bureau de change, restaurant and bar.

There are frequent daily flights from Madeira to the airport at **Porto Santo** (tel: 291-980 125). All these flights are operated by TAP Air Portugal (www.flytap.com). There are also some direct flights to Porto Santo from Lisbon and Oporto.

Where can I get a taxi? **Onde posso encontrar um táxi?**
How much is it to central Funchal? **Quanto custa para ir ao centro de Funchal?**
Does this bus go to Funchal? **Vai para Funchal este autocarro?**

B

BICYCLE HIRE

You can rent a mountain bike from **Bikezone** (tel: 291-636 891; www.bikezone.pt) at Rua Vale da Ajuda 100 in Funchal.

BUDGETING FOR YOUR TRIP

Getting to Madeira. There are regular scheduled and charter flights direct to Madeira (or via Lisbon) from many European cities. Return flights from London are likely to cost from £100–400. Economical package deals – flights and hotel included – are usually available.

Accommodation. Hotels at the top levels are comparable to those in large European cities. Many of the 2-, 3- and 4-star ratings are comparatively good value. A double room with bath per night in a cheaper hotel averages €50–100 and mid-range €100–150; while more luxurious options cost from €150 upwards.

Meals. Even top-rated restaurants may be surprisingly affordable compared to most European capitals. Portuguese wines are quite good and very attractively priced, even in fine restaurants. A three-course meal with wine in a reasonable establishment averages €20–50 per person. Many hotels offer half- and full-board plans.

Local transport. Buses and taxis are reasonable. A bus to the centre of Funchal from the hotel or tourist zone is about €1.60; a rechargeable Flexicard costs €2, which you can then use on repeated journeys; a taxi costs about €5 (add a fare supplement of 20 percent on weekends and public holidays between 10pm and 7am).

Incidentals. Your major expenses will be excursions, entertainment and sporting activities. Hiring a car allows greater flexibility, although if you enter the interior you will have to contend with challenging roads and steep ascents and descents. Economy hire costs from €35–€45 a day, including collision insurance and taxes. Petrol is around €1.80 a litre, diesel around €1.50.

Nightclub cover charges are high, and some clubs have a minimum consumption policy of around €150. A folklore or *fado* show, including dinner, run at €23–60 per person.

Coach trips around the island from Funchal cost €10–20. Island-hopping to Porto Santo by air is about €60 return; by ferry, €57 return.

C

CAMPING

There are two regular campsites on the Madeira archipelago, one in Porto Moniz and the other on Porto Santo, in Vila Baleira. A third, in the Montado do Pereiro nature reserve on the slopes above Funchal, requires prior permission and authorisation from the Madeira Camping service. For more detailed information contact: **Parque de Campismo do Porto Santo** (Vila Baleira, 9400 Porto Santo, Madeira; tel: 291-982 160) or the **Madeira Camping Service** (Estrada Monumental/Hotel Baía Azul; tel: 291-776 726; email: info@madeira-camping.com), or visit www.madeira-camping.com.

Is there a campsite near here? **Há algum parque de campismo por aqui perto?**
May we camp here? **Podemos acampar aqui?**

CAR HIRE (see also Driving, page 116 and Budgeting for Your Trip)

There are local and international car hire agencies in Funchal (most near the hotel and tourist zones) and at the airport. Prices vary significantly, so shop around – local firms tend to be cheaper and less prone to charging extra for scratches or dents.

You must be at least 21 and have held a valid national (or international) licence for at least a year. You need to present a recognised credit card when booking. Third-party fire and theft insurance is included in the basic charge. Check with your credit-card company before departure to verify what it covers when used to pay for the rental. Many will cover the collision damage waiver and theft of vehicle protection. A government tax of 12 percent is added to the total bill when booking locally.

An economy hire (such as a Nissan Micra) starts at €145 per week. Major international agents are: **Avis** (Largo António Nobre 164; tel: 291-764 546); **Europcar** (Estrada Monumental 306; tel: 291-765 116); **Hertz** (Estrada Monumental 284; tel: 291-764 410); and **Sixt** (Estrada Monumental 182; tel: 291-764 221).

I'd like to hire a car **Queria alugar um carro**
…tomorrow …**para amanhã**
…for one day/one week …**por um dia/uma semana**
Please include full insurance. **Que inclua um seguro contra todos os riscos, por favor**.

CLIMATE

Madeira is generally warm and spring-like all year, making it an excellent winter retreat for northern Europeans wishing to escape the cold and miserable weather. However, winter months can be rather wet and windy. The rainiest period is from October to December, with an average of six to seven days of rain per month, but even then you can usually count on an average of six hours sunshine each day. During the summer months, May to September, the air is warm and somewhat humid.

The typical pattern, year-round, is a clear, bright morning, with clouds rolling down from the mountains in the afternoon. For warm, clear weather, ideal for mountain walking, summer is your best bet. Average daily temperatures on Madeira are:

	J	F	M	A	M	J	J	A	S	O	N	D
min °C	13	13	13	14	16	17	19	19	19	18	16	14
max °C	19	18	19	19	21	22	24	24	24	23	22	19
min °F	56	56	56	58	60	63	66	67	67	65	61	58
max °F	66	65	66	67	69	72	75	74	76	74	71	67

CLOTHING

Light clothes are all you need in summer, but pack warm layers for mountain excursions. In winter a light, rainproof jacket may come in handy and you will definitely need warm, waterproof clothes for inland trips. If you are planning on walking you will obviously need sensible footwear, but unless you are intent on tackling some of the more arduous trails, you won't need hiking boots.

Madeira has long been a place where visitors dress up for tea and formal dinners. There is less formality these days – shorts and T-shirts are fine during the day – but Reid's formal restaurants still require men to wear a dark suit and tie. At other luxury hotels and restaurants, jacket and tie are generally expected. Nightspots such as the casino are more relaxed and jackets and ties are not required.

Will I need a tie? **É preciso gravata?**
Is it all right if I wear this? **Vou bem assim?**

CRIME AND SAFETY (see also Emergencies and Police)

Although Madeira is one of the safest places in the world for tourists, factors such as poverty (which does exist here, especially in small villages) inevitably make temptation irresistible for some, and there have been some problems with drug users mugging walkers along lonely *levada* trails. Follow the same general rules that you would elsewhere. Never leave anything of value in your car, even if it is out of sight. Burglaries of holiday apartments are rare, but leave any valuables in a safe-deposit box, or, in a hotel, with reception staff. You must report any losses to the police within 24 hours and get a copy of your statement for insurance purposes.

I want to report a theft. **Quero participar um roubo.**

D

DRIVING

There are several good reasons not to drive on Madeira: car hire and petrol are not cheap, but taxis are, and the tortuous mountain roads can be hard on one's nerves. Conversely, you may enjoy the challenge of the winding roads and, of course, a car gives maximum flexibility.

Road conditions. It is only worth considering driving into Funchal if you are staying well outside the town (at Machico or Garajau, for instance). If you do, expect traffic jams. The roads across the island offer a choice between fast modern highways, often enclosed in tunnels, or scenic but slow mountain roads that can be tortuously twisting. The latter demand confident, relaxed drivers.

Rules and regulations. The rules are the same as in the rest of Europe: drive on the right, overtake on the left, and give way to vehicles coming from the right. Speed limits are nominally 110kph (68mph) on highways, 90kph (56mph) outside built-up areas and 50kph (30mph) in built-up areas. Average speeds on country roads are well below 60kph (37mph). Seat belts must be worn at all times and children under the age of 12 are not allowed in front seats. Motorcyclists must always wear helmets.

Fuel costs. Unleaded petrol is around €1.80 per litre, diesel is around €1.50. Prices, controlled by the government, should be the same – or very similar – everywhere you go. Many petrol stations are open 24 hours a day, and all accept credit cards.

Road signs. Apart from the standard international pictographs, you may encounter the following:

If you need help. If you are driving a hired car, the hire company will give you a number to contact in case of breakdown or emergency. If you belong to a motoring organisation affiliated to the **Automóvel Clube de Portugal** (acp; www.pai.pt), you can make use of its services free of charge. The Funchal office is at Rua Dr António

Alto Stop
Cruzamento Crossroads
Curva perigosa Dangerous bend/curve
Descida íngreme Steep hill
Desvio Detour
Encruzilhada Crossing
Estacionamento permitido Parking permitted
Estacionamento proibido No parking
Guiar com cuidado Drive with care
Máquinas em manobras Men working
Obras/Trabalhos Men working
Paragem (de autocarro) Bus stop
Pare Stop
Pedestres, peões Pedestrians
Perigo Danger
Proibida a entrada No entry
Seguir pela direita/esquerda Keep right/left
Sem saída No through road

Are we on the right road for...? **É esta estrada para...?**
Fill it up, please, with... **Encha, por favor, de...**
three star/four star/unleaded/diesel **normal/super/sem
    chumbo/gasóleo**
My car's broken down **O meu carro está avariado**
There's been an accident **H ouve um acidente**

José Almeida 17-2°; tel: 291-223 659. You will have no problem finding well-equipped garages in Madeira.
Parking. Funchal is served by reasonably priced car parks at either
end of town. However, finding a parking space in the centre of town
is virtually impossible, except in the 'blue zone' (metered parking)
along Avenida do Mar e das Comunidades Madeirenses (facing the

Marina). You should have few difficulties parking your car elsewhere on the island.

E

ELECTRICITY

The standard current is 220-volt, 50Hz AC. For US appliances, 220v transformers and plug adaptors are needed.

I need an adaptor/a battery, please. **Preciso de um adaptador/uma pilha, por favor**.

EMBASSIES AND CONSULATES

Embassies of the following nations are in Lisbon:
UK (Embassy) Rua de São Bernardo 33, Lisbon; tel: 808 20 35 37 (00351 21 392 4153 if calling from outside Portugal); email: funchal. consulate@fco.gov.uk.
Australia (Embassy) Avenida da Liberdade 200, Lisbon; tel: 21310 1500.
Canada (Embassy/Consulate) Avenida da Liberdade 198–200, 3°, Lisbon; tel: 21-316 4600.
Republic of Ireland (Embassy/Consulate) Rua da Imprensa à Estrela 1–4, Lisbon; tel: 21-392 9440.
South Africa (Embassy) Avenida Luis Bívar 10, Lisbon; tel: 21-319 2200.
US (Embassy/Consulate) Avenida das Forças Armadas 16, Lisbon; tel: 21-727 2122.

Most embassies and consulates are open Mon–Fri 8am–noon and 2–4pm.

Where is the British embassy? **Onde é a embaixada inglesa?**

EMERGENCIES (see also Health and Medical Care, page 121)

The emergency number for police, fire or ambulance is **112**. Funchal hospital has a 24-hour emergency ward; tel: 291-705 666. Outside Funchal, ask for the local Centro de Saúde (Health Centre).

G

GAY AND LESBIAN TRAVELLERS

www.portugalgay.pt features a gay and lesbian travel guide, with information in English and other languages. It has little specific information relating to Madeira, but there is a message board for postings.

GETTING THERE (see also Airports)

Air Travel. There are frequent charter flights to Madeira from international and regional airports in the UK and from international airports in Austria, France, Germany, Spain and Scandinavia. The national Portuguese airline is TAP/Air Portugal (www. flytap. com), which flies from several European cities to Funchal, sometimes via Lisbon or Porto. For cheaper fares, check with easyJet (www.easyjet.com), for 'no-frills' flights to Funchal from Gatwick, London. The flight time from London to Madeira is approximately 3 hours 30 minutes, and from Lisbon to Madeira about 1 hour 30 minutes.

As well as these scheduled operators, many charter flights connect Madeira to mainland Europe and are much less expensive. Cruise liners stop off at the island, but often only for a brief tour.

GUIDES AND TOURS (see Public Transport)

A good way of seeing Madeira is by coach or minibus tour. Several operators go to the same places, but charge different rates for different services. Itineraries include: West of the Island; East of the Island, including Pico do Arieiro; a half-day covering Monte/Curral das Freiras/ Picos dos Barcelos; guided levada walks; and Jeep Safaris to out-of-the-way places such as Boca dos Namorados (see page 45) or Paúl da Serra (see page 50). Not all of these are good value; the Monte trip is simple and inexpensive to do by yourself (see page 41), as are the *levada* walks (see page 59). Other itineraries offer a day trip to Porto Santo, including an island tour (this is only recommended in summer, when sunshine and calm sailing are the norm), but you can also make your own way to the island and take a half-day minibus tour. Half-day boat trips cruise up and down the Madeiran coast, and other outings from Funchal Marina include a trip to the Ilhas Desertas, or a full day's sailing, including lunch and wine.

Information on tour operators, including Blandy's and other agencies, is available from the Funchal tourist office (see page 131) and most hotels. Particularly highly recommended are **Lido Tours** (18 Centro Commercial Monumental Lido; tel: 291- 635 505; www.lido-tours.com), which offers small island tours in minibuses, *levada* walks and mountain walks; guides speak multiple languages and tours are good value

Another recommended tour company is Windsor Travel (tel: 291-700 600; www.windsormadeira.com), which offers very well organised tours across the island, including to the viewing point at Pico dos Barcelos and to the island of Porto Santo.

Madeira Explorers focuses on guided outdoor ecotourism (Centro Commercial Monumental Lido, Shop 5, 3rd Floor; tel: 291-763 701; www.madeira-levada-walks.com). **Nature Meetings** specialises in guided walks, which you can do as part of a group, or individually, with transport provided at the start and end of the walk (tel: 291-

We'd like an English-speaking guide/an English interpreter.
Queremos um guia que fale inglês/um intérprete de inglês.

524 482; www.naturemeetings.com). **Terras de Aventura** organise adventure sports, including walking, canoeing, water sports, hang-gliding and mountain biking (Caminho do Amparo 25, Funchal; tel: 291-708 990; www.terrasdeaventura.com).

H

HEALTH AND MEDICAL CARE (see also Emergencies)

There are numerous health centres in Madeira and one on Porto Santo. *Farmácias* (chemists) are open Mon–Fri 9am–1pm, 3–7pm, Sat 9am–1pm. On the door of every pharmacy you will find postings of after-hours chemists.

Tourist offices carry lists of doctors and dentists who speak English. For more serious illness or injury, **Hospital Cruz de Carvalho** (Avenida Luis de Camoes 57; tel: 291 705 666) is the island's largest hospital and has English-speaking staff. In an emergency, dial **112** for an ambulance.

It is highly recommended that you take out travel insurance to cover any costs associated with illness or accidents while abroad. EU nationals with a European Health Insurance Card (EHIC), obtainable online at www.ehic.org.uk, can receive free emergency treatment at Social Security and Municipal hospitals. Private hospitals are expensive. If you don't take the EHIC card with you, you must pay on the spot and claim on your travel insurance later.

Where's the nearest (all night) pharmacy? **Onde fica a farmácia (de serviço) mais próxima?**
I need a doctor/dentist **Preciso de um médico/dentista**
an ambulance **uma ambulância**
hospital **hospital**
An upset stomach **Dôr de estômago**
Sunburn/a fever **Queimadura de sol/febre**

The most likely health problems will be due to an excess of sun or alcohol. Madeiran tap water (*água*) is safe and tastes pretty good. Bottled mineral water is sold everywhere.

Mosquitoes are present in summer, so it is worth buying an anti-mosquito device that plugs into your wall, available at airport shops.

HOLIDAYS

1 January **Ano Novo** New Year's Day
25 April **Dia da Liberdade** Freedom Day
1 May **Dia do Trabalho** Labour Day
10 June **Dia de Portugal** National Day
15 August **Assunção** Assumption
5 October **Dia da República** Republic Day
1 November **Todos os Santos** All Saints' Day
1 December **Restuaração/Dia da Independência** Day of Restoration/Independence
8 December **Imaculada Conceição** Immaculate Conception
25 December **Natal** Christmas Day
Movable dates:
Carnaval Shrove Tuesday/Carnival
Sexta-feira Santa Good Friday
Corpo de Cristo Corpus Christi

Madeira also celebrates 1 July (Madeira Autonomous Region Day), 21 August (municipal holiday) and 26 December (Boxing Day).

L

LANGUAGE

Madeira's official language is Portuguese. Basic Spanish should help with reading signs and menus, but is unlikely to unlock the mysteries of spoken Portuguese.

The *Berlitz Portuguese Phrasebook and Dictionary* covers most situations you are likely to encounter during a visit to Portugal. Also useful is the *Berlitz Portuguese–English/English–Portuguese Pocket Dictionary*, containing a special menu-reader supplement.

Good day/afternoon/evening **Bom dia/Boa tarde/Boa noite**
Goodbye **Adeus**
Please faz **favor (por favor)**
thank you **obrigado/obrigada (male/female speaker)**
How do you do/Pleased to meet you **Muito prazer**
How are you? **Como está?**
Very well, thank you **Muito bem, obrigado/obrigada**
What does this mean? **Que quer dizer isto?**
Please write it down **Escreva-mo, por favor**
where/when/how? **onde/quando/como?**
how long/how far? **quanto tempo/a que distância?**
left/right **esquerdo/direito**
cheap/expensive **barato/caro**
hot/cold **quente/frio**
old/new **velho/novo**
open/closed **aberto/fechado**
vacant/occupied **livre/ocupado**
early/late **cedo/tarde**
Help me, please **Ajude-me, por favor**
day/week/month/year **dia/semana/mês/ano**
yesterday/today/tomorrow **ontem/hoje/amanhã**
Sunday **domingo**
Monday **segunda-feira**
Tuesday **terça-feira**
Wednesday **quarta-feira**
Thursday **quinta-feira**
Friday **sexta-feira**
Saturday **sábado**
What day is it today? **Que dia é hoje?**

M

MAPS

Madeira is a small island with relatively few roads, so orientation is easy. The tourist offices in Funchal and Porto Santo can supply a free map that includes the island and capital and shows several of the most popular *levada* trails. For almost all purposes, even driving across the whole island, the free map should be sufficient, but more detailed maps are published by the Instituto Geográfico e Cadastral, obtainable at local bookshops. Few maps are up to date because of the rapid pace of road building. The best map available in the UK is the Madeira Tour and Trail Map, www.walking. demon.co.uk. Those intent on serious walking should buy a copy of *Landscapes of Madeira* by John and Pat Underwood (Sunflower Books; www.sunflowerbooks.co.uk), which includes specially drawn walking tour maps and details many *levada* trails. Their Walk & Eat Madeira is aimed at those on shorter trips, but also contains detailed walking trails.

MEDIA

Europe's principal papers, including most British dailies, are on the newsstands the day after publication. Popular foreign magazines are sold at many kiosks. The only local English-language publication is the free monthly, *The Madeira Island Bulletin* (www.mib.criacoes. com; also available in German as *Madeira Aktuell*). You can pick up a copy at the tourist office in Funchal. If you can understand a little Portuguese, the daily *Notícias da Madeira* (www.dnoticias.pt) newspaper gives you a weather forecast and details of museum and temporary exhibitions, among other things.

Madeira has its own TV channel and also receives programmes from mainland Portugal. Most large hotels and some bars also have satellite TV for screening football matches and other sporting events. For details of what's on, pick up a copy of the *Notícias da Madeira*.

The BBC World Service and Voice of America can be heard on shortwave radio.

Have you any English-ianguage newspapers/magazines? **Tem jornais/ revistas em inglês?**

MONEY (see also Budgeting for Your Trip)

Currency. The euro is the official currency used in Portugal. Notes are denominated in 5, 10, 20, 50, 100 and 500 euros; coins in 1 and 2 euros and 1, 2, 5, 10, 20 and 50 cents.

Currency exchange. Normal banking hours are Mon–Fri 8.30am–3pm. Some banks remain open later and at weekends to change money. There is also a 24-hour bureau de change at the airport. Banks either levy up to 12 percent in commission or charge a flat fee of around £15/US$20, regardless of the amount, so ask first. Automatic machines are the easiest method of obtaining euros and provide by far the best exchange rates.

Credit cards. Standard international credit cards are widely accepted, except in some shops and restaurants, especially in small villages.

Can I pay with this credit card? **Posso pagar com cartão de crédito?**
I want to change some pounds/dollars. **Queria trocar libras/ dólares.**
Can you cash a traveller's cheque? **Pode pagar um cheque de viagem?**
Where's the nearest bank/ currency exchange office? **Onde fica o banco mais próximo/a casa de câmbio mais próxima?**
How much is that? **Quanto custa isto?**

O

OPENING HOURS

Most businesses close for a one- to two-hour lunch break. Shops and offices are generally open 9am–1pm, 3–7pm Mon–Fri, and 9am–1pm Sat. Banks are open 8.30am–3pm, Mon–Fri, while some also open Sat 9am–1pm. Currency exchange offices generally open 9am–1pm and 2–7pm Mon–Fri, 9am–1pm Sat.

Most museums open from 10am–5pm Tue–Fri, although some close from 12.30–2pm, and some open at weekends, especially during summer. Café-restaurants may be open all day, whereas more up-market establishments close after lunch and reopen for dinner.

P

POLICE (see also Emergencies)

The national police, identified by their blue uniforms, are generally helpful and friendly and often speak a little English. If you need help or find yourself in an emergency situation, dial 112. The main police station in Funchal, where there is a lost property section, is on Rua João de Deus 7; tel: 291-222 022.

Where's the nearest police station? **Onde fica o posto de polícia mais próximo?**
I've lost… my wallet/bag/passport **Perdi... a minha carteira/o meu saco/o meu passaporte**

POST OFFICES (see also Telephones)

Post offices are indicated by the letters CTT (*Correios, Telégrafos e Telefones*). Mailboxes are painted bright red for second-class post and blue (*Correio Azul*) for first-class (next day delivery). Some post offices have separate slots for mail to the Portuguese mainland or international mail. The main post office in Funchal is on Avenida Zarco between Avenida Arriaga and Rua Carreira. It is open Mon–Fri 8.30am–8pm, Sat 9.30am–1pm. Local branches have shorter opening hours. You can buy stamps from tobacconists and kiosks, as well as at post offices.

Worldwide postage of a letter or postcard weighing up to 20g costs €1.80. Mail may take up to a week to reach a European destination.

Where's the nearest post office? **Onde fica a estação de correios mais próxima?**
express (special delivery) **expresso**
registered **registrado**

PUBLIC TRANSPORT

Buses. Most of the island is served by public buses, which are cheap, reliable and generally punctual. For those with the luxury of time and patience, it is possible to go almost anywhere that coach tours visit by public bus – a much cheaper but more time-consuming alternative. The tourist office sells a booklet giving details of bus services and routes. Bus stops are indicated by the sign *paragem*.

The two largest bus operators are SAM and Rodoeste. They have their main departure points on the Avenida do Mar e das Comunidades Madeirenses. You will find them between the Palácio de São Lourenço and the Zona Velha (Old Town).

Note that some intra-city and inter-city buses have identical numbers – for example, the orange town bus No. 20 to Monte is not the same as the green/cream island bus No. 20 to Santo da Serra.

Bus companies in Funchal have introduced a Giro card system, which costs €0.50 from automatic machines around the city or from authorised sellers. These cards are rechargeable, like the London Oyster cards, and need to be validated when you get on the bus.

Various charges apply, depending on the number of zones travelled; the simplest and best deal is the €15.90 7-day pass. Children under-6 travel free and those aged 6–16 qualify for reduced fares.

Taxi. Metered taxis – which cannot be hailed in the street but are found at ranks all over Funchal and in every town – are reasonably priced and convenient for most trips within Funchal and to sights just outside the city, such as Monte, the Botanical Garden and the Quinta do Palheiro. For many popular tourist trips, there is a government-set flat fare, which, by law, has to be displayed inside the taxi. Otherwise, the meter begins at €2. From the city centre to the hotel zone, expect to pay about €5. From the hotel zone to the airport costs around €20. All taxi rates are 20 percent higher after 10pm and at weekends and holidays.

Many people hire taxis as substitutes for coach tours. If several people are travelling, this can be a good deal. (Most taxis will charge about €60–80 per half day or €100–120 for a full day.) A list of popular excursions and prices is kept at the tourist office, or see Taxi Madeira (www.taximadeira.com)

Cable car. A cable car connects Funchal's Zona Velha (Old Town) to Monte, in the mountains above the city, and takes approximately 15 minutes. Another cable car connects Monte to the Botanical Garden.

Where is the nearest bus stop? **Onde é a paragem de auto-carros mais próxima?**
When's the next bus to...? **Quando parte o próximo autocarro para...?**
I want a ticket to... **Queria um bilhete para...**
single/return **ida/ida e volta**
Will you tell me when to get off? **Pode dizer-me quando devo descer?**
Where can I get a taxi? **Onde posso encontrar um táxi?**
What's the fare to...? **Quanto custa um bilhete para...?**

Flights to Porto Santo. Porto Santo can be reached easily several times a day by small aircraft from Madeira airport (tap, tel: 291-239 211). Flight time approximately 15 minutes, from about €60 return. **Ferry to Porto Santo**. The Porto Santo Line (Rua da Praia 6; tel: 291-210 300) operates a cruise-style ferry that departs from Funchal's harbour daily at 8am, and takes about 2 hours. It leaves Porto Santo at 6pm and costs around $57 return. (In winter the timetable is slightly reduced.) The new ships are far more stable than the old but travel pills are recommended for anyone prone to seasickness.

T

TELEPHONES

Portugal's country code is 351. Within Madeira, the local area code, 291, must be dialled, even for local calls (nine digits in total).

A few Portugal Telecom public telephones take coins, but most accept only prepaid phonecards. Payphones are found all over Madeira. *Credifone* phonecards can be purchased at post offices or at newspaper kiosks. Local, national and international calls can also be made from hotels, but with a substantial surcharge. Use an international calling card, if you must make a phone call from your hotel room.

To make an international call, dial 00 for an international line + the country code (eg UK 0044, US 001) + phone number (including the area code, without the initial '0' where there is one).

Dial 099 for the international operator for Europe, and 098 for the rest of the world. For directory enquiries in Madeira, dial 118.

Madeira has good mobile phone network coverage. International

A phone card, please **Um credifone, por favor**
Where's the pay phone? all **Onde está o telefone pago?**
My phone doesn't work here **O meu telefone não funciona aqui.**

charges differ according to your provider, so check these before you go to avoid any unpleasantly huge bills on your return. If your GSM phone is unlocked (which you can have done locally), you may use a local pay-as-you-go SIM card for cheaper local calls, which you can buy from provider networks, Vodafone, TMN or Optimus.

TIME

Madeira operates both winter (GMT + 0) and summer (GMT + 1) time periods, so Madeira is on the same time as the UK. From the last Sunday in March until the last Sunday in October, the clocks are moved one hour ahead. Times in summer are:

Sydney	**Madeira**	London	Los Angeles	New York
9pm	**noon**	noon	4am	7am

TIPPING

Hotel and restaurant bills are generally inclusive, but an additional tip of 5–10 percent is common and even expected in restaurants. Hotel wages are not high, and tips help to boost staff income: porters generally receive €1 a bag, the maid who cleans your room €1 a day. Taxi drivers do not expect a tip except for any special services.

TOILETS

Public toilets in Funchal are rare, and not usually recommended. The best place to find a clean toilet is in a large hotel or a restaurant or bar (out of courtesy you should buy a drink, or at least ask permission). 'Ladies' is marked *Senhoras* and 'Gents' *Homens* or *Senhores*. *Senhoras* and *Senhores* are easily confused.

Where are the toilets please? **¿Por favor, onde é o quarto de banho?**

TOURIST INFORMATION

Portugal does not have national tourist offices as such. Instead it maintains a website, Visit Portugal (www.visitportugal.com), from which various brochures can be ordered. In addition, Madeira has its own website – Madeira Tourism (www.visitmadeira.pt) – with plenty of information. If none of these sources is able to answer your questions, you could try contacting the following offices of ICEP (*Investimentos, Comércio e Turismo de Portugal*).

Canada: Suite 1005, 60 Bloor Street West, Toronto, Ontario M4W 3B8; tel: 416-921 7376.

South Africa: 5th Floor, Mercantile Lisbon House, 142 West Street, Sandown 2196, Johannesburg; tel: 2711-302 0404.

UK: Portuguese Embassy, 11 Belgrave Square, London SW1X 8PP; tel: 020-7235 5331; email:londres@mne.pt

US: 590 Fifth Ave, 4th floor, New York, NY10036; tel: 646-723 0299.

The Regional Department of Tourism in Madeira has 10 offices. The tourist information office in Funchal, the most dependable, is at Avenida Arriaga 18; tel: 291-211 900; info@madeiratourism.com. It is open Mon–Fri 9am–8pm, Sat–Sun 9am–6pm. The airport tourist office (tel: 291-524 933) is open daily 9am–8pm. Provincial offices in Caniço, Machico, Ribeira Brava, Câmara de Lobos, Porto Moniz, Santana and Porto Santo keep normal business hours, though most close for lunch and some of them do not always open in the afternoon.

V

VISAS AND ENTRY REQUIREMENTS

To visit Portugal, UK citizens, Americans, Canadians and people of many other nationalities do not need a visa, just a passport valid for six months. EU nationals (except those from the UK) may enter with an identity card. The length of stay authorised for most tourists is 90 days (60 for US and Canadian citizens).

Currency restrictions. Visitors from abroad may bring into Portugal (or depart with) any amount of euros or foreign currency.

Customs. Madeira is part of the EU, but has separate duty-free status within Portugal. You can import the following amounts duty-free: 200 cigarettes or 50 cigars or 250g of tobacco; 1 litre of spirits; 2 litres of wine; 50g of perfume and 250ml of eau de toilette.

W

WEBSITES AND INTERNET CAFÉS

www.madeira-island.com A periodic webzine with events, chat room and links to travel providers, hotels, etc.

www.madeira-web.com Run by a commercial travel agent, in English, German, Spanish and Portuguese, with a guide to outdoor activities, island tours and property.

www.visitmadeira.pt A helpful site with lots of up-to-date travel information, published by the Madeira Board of Tourism.

www.madeiraapartments.com A guide to self-catering accommodation on Madeira as an alternative to hotels.

www.madeirawine.com Information on local wines and an e-shop.

Y

YOUTH HOSTELS

There are three official youth hostels in Madeira: at Calçada da Cabouqueira 5 in Funchal, tel: 291-741 540; at Sítio dos Serrões Acima in Calheta, tel: 291-822 500; and at Vila do Porto Moniz in Porto Moniz, tel: 291-853 915; plus one on Porto Santo at Sítio das Matas, tel: 291-982 607.

Visit the website of the International Youth Hostelling Federation at www.hihostels.com for further information.

Recommended Hotels

The choice of hotel accommodation on Madeira is wider than ever. Traditional hotels are clustered in the hotel and tourist zones hugging the coast west of Funchal. Many of these have been updating their design and services to compete with newer hotels in the *zona turista*. At the same time, hotel accommodation across the island is rapidly being expanded, and visitors can choose from hotels, *quintas* (villas), *estalagens* and *pousadas* (inns) along the coast and in the villages and mountains of the interior.

Book especially early for Christmas and New Year (when most hotels charge a huge supplement) and for smaller hotels throughout the year. Otherwise, high season rates generally apply from Easter through May and July to the end of September. Price guidelines below are for a double room with bath in high season, including breakfast and VAT (value-added tax). All hotels accept major credit cards. For making reservations, Portugal's country code is 351; the area code, 291, is the same throughout Madeira and must always be dialled.

€€€€	over 200 euros
€€€	150–200 euros
€€	100–150 euros
€	below 100 euros

FUNCHAL TOWN

Castanheiro € *Rua do Castanheiro 27, 9000 Funchal; tel: 291-227 060*. Good-value apartments in an excellent location just off Praça do Município. Well-equipped rooms and friendly staff. The adjacent snack-bar restaurant is recommended. 32 apartments.

Porto Santa Maria €€€ *Avenida do Mar e das Comunidades Madeirenses 50, 9060-190 Funchal; tel: 291-206 700; www.portobay.com.* Located on the seafront in the Old Town, close to the cable car and next door to the 17th-century São Tiago fortress. The rooms are modern, and some studio apartments are also available. There is a heated indoor pool, restaurant and two bars. Disabled access. 146 rooms.

Quinta da Bela Vista €€€€ *Caminho do Avista Navios 4, 9000 Funchal; tel: 291-706 400;* www.belavistamadeira.com. A plush hotel at the eastern end of the Old Town, built around an elegant 19th-century mansion, with splendid views and a lovely garden. The beautiful rooms are furnished with antiques. Excellent food at the formal restaurant. Small gym and sauna, swimming pool and library. 67 rooms.

Santa Maria € *Rua João de Deus 26, 9050 Funchal; tel: 291-225 271.* Simple hotel in the Old Town, close to some excellent restaurants. Rooftop swimming pool with lovely views over Funchal and the sea. 83 rooms.

Windsor €€ *Rua das Hortas 4, 9050 Funchal; tel: 291-233 081;* www.hotelwindsorgroup.pt. Hotel Windsor Group is a chain of three hotels located in the centre of Funchal: The Windsor Hotel, Hotel do Centro and Residencial Greco. They have all been refurbished and are a good choice for those who want to be housed in the heart of the city. 67 rooms.

FUNCHAL HOTEL ZONE

Aparthotel Imperatriz € *Rua da Imperatriz Dona Amélia 72, 9000 Funchal; tel: 291-233 456;* www.sousahotels.com. Surrounded by luxury hotels, and adjacent to the Casino, these studio apartments, all with kitchenette and balcony, have a rooftop swimming pool with views of the sea. A good choice for those on a tight budget. 27 studios.

Avenue Park Apartamentos Turísticos €€ *Avenida do Infante 26, 9000 Funchal; tel: 291-205 630;* www.avenuepark-madeira.com. Smart, modern apartments (studios and one- and two-bedroom apartments) located across from the Santa Catarina Park and the Casino, and no more than a five-minute walk from Funchal's city centre. They are fashionably equipped with modern furnishings in bright colours and nice, clean kitchenettes. Disabled access. 15 apartments.

Cliff Bay Hotel €€€€ *Estrada Monumental 147, 9004-532 Funchal; tel: 291-707 700; www.portobay.com.* This luxurious hotel is set on a clifftop opposite the Lido supermarket, with panoramic sea and harbour views from nearly all its rooms. Guests are pampered with large, smartly designed rooms, and spacious and well-equipped bathrooms. The main facilities include two swimming pools (one of them a seawater lagoon), a spa, a tennis court, three restaurants and four bars. Disabled access. Free Wi-fi. 200 rooms and suites.

Madeira Regency Club €€€ *Rua Carvalho Araújo 9, 9000-022 Funchal; tel: 291-205 757; www.regency-hotels-resorts.com.* Spacious and well-equipped poolside apartments with sun terraces and access to the sea. Heated seawater pool and children's pool. Most rooms overlook the sea and harbour. The staff are exceptionally friendly. Other facilities include a sauna and squash courts. Disabled access. 96 rooms.

Penha de França €€ *Rua da Imperatriz Dona Amélia 85, 9000 Funchal; tel: 291-724 273; www.penhafranca.com.* A restored manor house (*albergaria*) tucked away in a lovely garden in the midst of Funchal's hotel district. Although small and intimate, it nevertheless has a piano bar, outdoor dining, a lawn and a pool with an expansive terrace and terrific sea views. Stylish rooms. Disabled access. 76 rooms.

Pestana Carlton Madeira €€€€ *Largo António Nobre, 9000 Funchal; tel: 291-239 500; www.pestana.com.* Attractive, luxurious 5-star complex sitting on a clifftop overlooking Funchal Bay. The hotel spans a river gorge with direct views of the sea. The rooms are large and comfortable, and all have balconies. Four restaurants and lively nightlife, as well as a tennis court, two swimming pools (one of which is a saltwater pool with direct access to the ocean), diving school and other sports facilities. Package deals are available. Disabled access. 375 rooms.

Pestana Casino Park €€€€ *Rua da Imperatriz Dona Amélia 55, 9000 Funchal; tel: 291-209 100; www.pestana.com.* Large 1960s concrete complex (designed by the great Brazilian architect Oscar Niemeyer) set within its own gardens overlooking the coast and Funchal's harbour. It takes the resort part of its name seriously, with a large swimming pool, activities and nightly entertainment at the adjacent casino and nightclubs. The tastefully furnished rooms all have balconies. Slightly less expensive than competing 5-star hotels. Disabled access. 327 rooms.

Quinta Perestrello €€€ *Rua Dr Pita 3, 9000 Funchal; tel: 291-775 936; www.quintaperestrellomadeira.com.* Delightful 150-year-old country house with period antiques, a lovely garden and swimming pool. Located close to Quinta do Magnolia park, but adjacent to a busy road junction, so some rooms can be subject to traffic noise. The restaurant serves light meals, but guests can also use all the facilities at sister hotels in the Charming Hotels Madeira group. 36 rooms.

Reid's Palace €€€€ *Estrada Monumental 139, 9000 Funchal; tel: 291-717 171 (from US and Canada tel: 800 237 1236, toll-free; from UK tel: 0845-077 2222, local call rate); www.reidspalace.com.* Madeira's legendary hotel is a magnificent mansion that preserves the elegance of an earlier era. Sumptuously decorated, the hotel has magnificent gardens overlooking the sea, spacious sun terraces, pools and tennis courts. A wide variety of packages is available, some of them surprisingly affordable at certain times of the year. Disabled access. 173 rooms.

Savoy Resort €€€€ *Avenida do Infante, 9004 Funchal; tel: 291-213 000; www.savoyresort.com.* Two great hotels under one management. The Savoy Hotels & Resorts Madeira comprises the luxurious 5-star Royal Savoy (174 bedrooms) and the superior 4-star Savoy Gardens (Azinhaga da Casa Branca, 9004-543, Funchal; tel: 291-724 226; 119 bedrooms). The first is situated in Funchal's premium location, directly on the oceanfront with a magnificent sea-level solarium area of lush subtropical gardens with direct sea access, fountains, water cascades and swimming pools. All rooms have their own private balcony and panoramic views. The superior 4-star Savoy Gardens, a boutique-style hotel, is located in a quiet and sunny suburb of the city. It has a reading room with a library, and an extensive panoramic rooftop terrace complete with whirlpool. After dark there is nightly musical entertainment. On the site of the former legendary Classic Savoy Hotel, which has been demolished, the group is in the process of building the new Hotel Savoy (350 bedrooms), though a completion date is not available at the tie of printing.

FUNCHAL TOURIST ZONE

CS Madeira Atlantic Resort & Sea Spa €€€€ *Estrada Monumental 175–7, 9000 Funchal; tel: 291-717 600;* www.cs-madeira.com. The CS Madeira Atlantic Resort & Sea Spa is formed of two towers separated by a low block with a wave-shaped roof. The decor is minimalist and stylish, and all rooms have panoramic sea views. Three restaurants, lively bars, two indoor and four outdoor pools, a spa, tennis and squash courts, and a fitness centre. Disabled access. 300 rooms.

Hotel Girassol €€€ *Estrada Monumental 256, 9004 Funchal; tel: 291-701 570;* http://hotelgirassolmadeira.com. The Girassol is a modern hotel, pleasant and friendly, with a consistent package-deal clientele. The rooms are fairly basic, but each one has a terrace or balcony overlooking the garden, the mountains or the sea. Despite being located right on the busy main Funchal highway, the hotel has a secluded garden full of shady spots to recline in, poolside bar, two swimming pools (one of them heated), plus children's paddling pools. It also has a restaurant, which has sea views and, at dinner, there is live music. Disabled access. 133 rooms.

Pensão Vila Vicência € *Rua da Casa Branca 45, 9000 Funchal; tel: 291-771 527;* www.vilavicencia.com. A delightful, family-run *pension* comprising three adjacent houses, Vila Vicência is just a five-minute walk from the Lido complex. Rooms are simply yet tastefully furnihed, some with balconies, and it has a lovely little garden with a private swimming pool. 29 rooms.

Pestana Palms €€€ *Rua do Gorgulho 17, 9000 Funchal; tel: 291-709 200;* www.pestana.com. This aparthotel on the seafront incorporates a refurbished *quinta*. All the rooms are nicely furnished, self-catering studios. Heated pool, health club, gymnasium and special touches including a diving club and school, and free internet use. 167 rooms.

Pestana Village €€€ *Estrada Monumental 194, 9000 Funchal; tel: 291-701 600;* www.pestana.com. Looking rather like a well-designed village straight out of a Mexican resort, the Village Aparthotel has a faux-Moorish lobby with a mosaic floor, a beautifully landscaped swimming pool area and award-winning subtropical gardens with native trees. Nicely equipped studio apartment suites and a relaxing spa centre. Half-board is available. Disabled access. 200 rooms.

Suite Hotel Eden Mar €€€ *Rua do Gorgulho 2, 9004-537, Funchal; tel: 291-709 700;* www.portobay.pt. This is a well-equipped, popular, and modern aparthotel set in a busy location in the heart of the tourist zone. Part of the Eden Mar shopping complex, with shops, bars and restaurants on the doorstep. All studios have a kitchenette, private balcony and sea views. Guests have access to outdoor and indoor pools set in lush gardens, as well as squash, snooker, a health club, a spa and sauna, a sun terrace, a pleasant garden, four restaurants and six bars. Disabled access. 146 studios and rooms.

Tivoli Madeira €€€€ *Rua Simplício dos Passos Gouveia 29, 9004-576 Funchal; tel: 291-702 000;* www.tivolihotels.com. Formerly known as the Tivoli Ocean Park, this is another of the big and bold 5-star hotels to sprout along the coast in the tourist zone. It is awash with sports facilities, and all the expected comforts and services, and the modern rooms, which all have balconies and sea views, are extremely plush. The hotel runs a bus service to Funchal Marina. Disabled access. 317 rooms.

BEYOND FUNCHAL

Casa das Videiras € *Sítio Serra d'Água, 9270 Seixal; tel: 291-222 667;* www.casa-das-videiras.com. Charming guesthouse in a tiny, pretty town on the north coast. The mid-19th-century manor house has clean and attractively decorated rooms, and the atmosphere is very friendly and relaxed – a tribute to the hands-on owner. Self-catering possible. Deals available: seven nights for the price of six, 14 nights for the price of 12. 4 rooms.

Casa do Caseiro € *Caminho do Monte 62, 9050 Funchal; tel: 291-611 031;* www.acasadocaseiro.com. Friendly hotel located high above Funchal, halfway down Monte's famous toboggan run. Small, delightful, private house, attractive gardens, pool and terrace with lovely views. 7 rooms.

Casa Velha do Palheiro €€€€ *Rua da Estalagem 23, São Gonçalo, 9060 Funchal; tel: 291-790 350;* www.casa-velha.com. Nestled in the hills east of Funchal, with great views of the city, this handsome and stylish inn occupies a beautiful 1804 country-estate house connected to the Palheiro Gardens. Part of the prestigious Palheiro Golf Club (special golf packages available) – it's the only hotel in Madeira on a golf course – and with an elegant restaurant, heated pool, gym and tennis court. 37 rooms.

Choupana Hills Resort €€€€ *Travessa do Largo da Choupana, 9060-348 Funchal; tel: 291-206 020;* www.choupanahills.com. Catering for international jet-setting clients, the Choupana Hills combines Balinese-style timber bungalows with all mod cons, and lush sub-tropical gardens watered by *levada*, which you can follow westwards to Monte or eastwards to the Palheiro Gardens. Alternatively, laze in the hotel's large and well-equipped spa, and enjoy casual all-day dining on local specialities or fusion food in the excellent Xôpana restaurant. 62 rooms.

Dom Pedro Baía €€€ *Estrada de São Roque, 9200 Machico; tel: 291-724 215;* www.dompedrobaiahotel.com. A modern high-rise overlooking the bay of Machico, this comfortable hotel is a good base for exploring the eastern part of the island. Popular with British and German package tours, it has an Olympic-size swimming pool, a tennis court, bar and nightly entertainment. Disabled access. 218 rooms.

Estalagem da Ponta do Sol €€ *Quinta da Rochinha, 9360 Ponta do Sol; tel: 291-970 200;* www.pontadosol.com. Another modern boutique hotel that undermines the image of Madeira as a resort for the retired, the Ponta do Sol is a Modernist dream, consisting of a series of white-walled cubes with plate-glass windows, set on the clifftop east of Ponta do Sol village. The delightful gardens and bar are located in the original mansion, while the excellent restaurant is perfectly positioned for glorious views of the sunset. 54 rooms.

Estalagem do Mar € *Sítio dos Juncos, Fajã da Areia, 9240 São Vicente; tel: 291-840 010;* www.hotelestalagemdomar. Within walking distance of São Vicente, sandwiched between a sheer cliff and the roaring sea, this sprawling hotel offers exclusivity at a bargain price. All the simply furnished rooms face the ocean. There is an indoor and outdoor pool, restaurant and tennis court. 99 rooms.

Estalagem Eira do Serrado €€€ *Eira do Serrado, Curral das Freiras, 9000 Funchal; tel: 291-710 060;* www.eiradoserrado.com. This 4-star guesthouse with elegant rooms, all with balconies, occupies a splendid setting right on the rim of the hidden valley of Curral das Freiras. Enchanting views are guaranteed as you look down over green terraces to the isolated village in the valley far below, or up to the jagged volcanic peaks that encircle the skyline. Games room, restaurant, jacuzzi, sauna and wine cellar. 25 rooms.

Estalagem Quinta do Estreito €€€€ *Rua José Joaquim da Costa, 9325 Estreito de Câmara de Lobos; tel: 291-775 936;* www.quintado estreitomadeira.com. A luxury *quinta*, or villa, with elegant furnishings set 400m (1,300ft) above sea level, overlooking the vineyards of Câmara de Lobos. A relaxing hideaway, the *quinta* has landscaped tropical gardens, restaurant, library and heated pool. Comfortable, tastefully decorated rooms. 48 rooms.

Pousada dos Vinháticos €€ *Fajã dos Vinháticos, Serra d'Água, 9350 Ribeira Brava; tel: 291-952 344;* www.pousadadosvinhaticos.com. This chalet-style inn – owned by the Dorisol hotel group, not by the Portuguese government as *pousadas* are on the mainland – is a terrific mountain refuge, ideal for nature enthusiasts and those in search of serenity. The inn is set in a splendid wood-cabin lodge (imported from Finland) with unmatched views and comfortable rooms. Good-value restaurant, games room and very friendly, knowledgeable staff. 21 rooms.

Quinta do Furão €€ *Achada do Gramacho, 9230 Santana; tel: 291-570 100;* www.quintadofurao.com. Newly built in rustic style, this rural inn is set amid a sea of green orchards and grapevines, with views of the undulating hills around Santana. The best hotel in the area, the 'Quinta of the Ferret' offers style and relaxation, with a cool little pool with a retractable roof, and a fine rustic restaurant. The hotel hosts a wine festival in September. 45 rooms and suites.

Residencial Amparo € *Rua da Amargura, 9200 Machico; tel: 291-968 120;* www.residencialamparo.web.pt. A simple hotel, comfortably decorated in contemporary style, located in the centre of Machico, just two blocks from the seafront. A pleasant and personal alternative to the larger Dom Pedro (see page 139). Attractive restaurant with outdoor seating in fine weather. 12 rooms.

Residencial Encumeada € *Feiteiras, Serra d'Água, 9350 Ribeira Brava; tel: 291-951 281;* www.residencialencumeada.com. Few places can match the setting of this unpretentious hotel. Just down the road from the Encumeada pass, it sits on a ledge overlooking the mountains and valley around Serra de Água, halfway between the north and south coasts. Ideal for walkers and hikers. 50 rooms.

PORTO SANTO

Torre Praia €€€ *Rua Goulart Medeiros, 9400 Porto Santo; tel: 291-980 450;* www.torrepraia.pt. Just outside Vila Baleira, this attractive 4-star hotel has simple furnishings and overlooks Porto Santo's excellent beach and the ocean. Kidney-shaped swimming pool, squash court, gym, sauna and jacuzzi, games room and three restaurants. 63 rooms.

INDEX

Berlitz pocket guide
Madeira

Sixth Edition 2014

Written by Neil Schlecht
Updated by Abigail Blasi
Edited by Carine Tracanelli
Picture Editor: Tom Smyth
Art Editor: Shahid Mahmood
Series Editor: Tom Stainer
Production: Tynan Dean and Rebeka Davies

Photography credits: 123RF 10, 26, 51; Alamy
78; Berlitz 67; Bigstock 47; Chris Coe/Apa
Publications 17, Corbis 2ML, 42, 82, Dreamstime
3T, 6TL, 8, 19, 35, 36, 55, 66, 71; Fotolia 2TL, 2MC,
3M, 3M, 7MC, 7TC, 12, 15, 29, 32, 49, 53, 56, 58,
69, 75, 76, 86; Glyn Genin/Apa Publications 68;
iStock 2/3M, 6ML, 7B, 30, 45, 46, 61, 84, 90, 91,
92, 96, 98; Madeira Tourism 2/3M, 4ML, 4ML,
4MR, 4TL, 4TL, 4/5M, 5MC, 4/5T, 5TC, 28, 39, 44,
50, 52, 62, 63, 72, 74, 81, 88; Madeira Tourism/
Julio Marques 33; Mary Evans Picture Library 21,
24; Orient-Express Hotels 95; Paul Murphy/Apa
Publications 3TC; Phil Wood/Apa Publications 1,
2TC, 6ML, 23, 64, 65, 101; Robert Harding 40

Cover picture: Dreamstime

Every effort has been made to provide
accurate information in this publication,
but changes are inevitable. The publisher
cannot be responsible for any resulting
loss, inconvenience or injury.

Contact us

At Berlitz we strive to keep our guides as
accurate and up to date as possible, but if you
find anything that has changed, or if you have
any suggestions on ways to improve this guide,
then we would be delighted to hear from you.

Berlitz Publishing, PO Box 7910,
London SE1 1WE, England.
email: berlitz@apaguide.co.uk
www.insightguides.com/berlitz

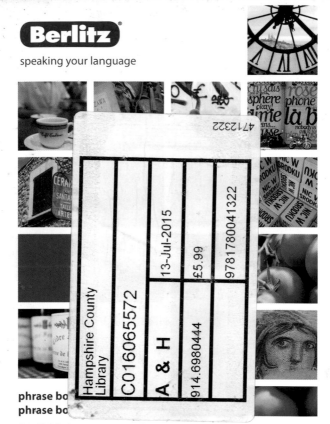

Berlitz®

speaking your language

phrase bo
phrase bo

Available in: Arabic, Brazilian Portuguese*, Burmese*, Cantonese Chinese, Croatian, Czech*, Danish*, Dutch, English, Filipino, Finnish*, French, German, Greek, Hebrew*, Hindi*, Hungarian*, Indonesian, Italian, Japanese, Korean, Latin American Spanish, Malay, Mandarin Chinese, Mexican Spanish, Norwegian, Polish, Portuguese, Romanian*, Russian, Spanish, Swedish, Thai, Turkish, Vietnamese
*Book only

www.berlitzpublishing.com

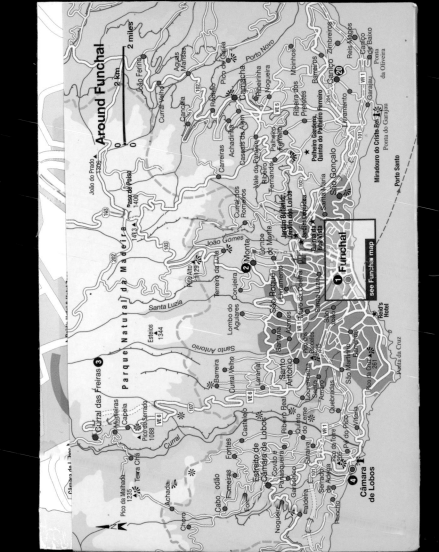

Around Funchal

2 km
2 miles

Pico da Malhada
1235

Achada

Curral

Cabo
odão
meiras
Fontes

Choro

Nogueira
Garacho

Faldeira

Serrado
de Açuga

Pasacho

Foi

Murteiras
Capela

Curral das Freiras ③

Picodo Serrado
1088

VE 6

Parque Natural da Madeira

Estelos
1344

João do Prado
1305

Casa de Poiso
1400

103

Santa Luzia

202

Pico Alto
1129

1413
João Gomes

103

Terreiro da Luta

Conjuria

② Monte

João Ferino

Currral Velho

Águas Mansas

Pico da Saúde

Porto Novo

Ribeiro Frio

Cancela

Camacha

Ribeirinha
Nogueira

VE 6

Achadinha

Carreiras

Casades das Alen

Curral dos
Romeiros

Lombo
do Monte

Vale do Paraíso
Ribeiro
Fernando

Palheiro
Ferreiro

Palheiro Gardens,
Quinta do Palheiro Ferreiro

Ribeira dos
Prefetés

Barreiros

Moinhos

Livramento

Garajau

VR 1

Caniço
② Zimbreiros

Reis Magos

Caniço
de Baxo

Ponta
da Oliveira

Ponta do Garajau

Miradouro do Cristo-Rei

Porto Santo

Bareira
Curral Velho
Laranjal

Lombo do
Aguiares

Santo Antonio

VE 6

Estreito de
Câmara de Lobos

Picodo Serrado
1088

Castelejo

Covão ⑥
Panasqueira

Ribeiro Real

Quinto

Salvato
do Leme

VR 1

Vitoria

Pe do Pico
1016

Serrado

Câmara
de Lobos ④

São Roque

Santa Maria

Livramento

Loureçanha
Santo
Amaro

Quebradas

Pico da Cruz
261

Porta da Cruz

Santo
Antonio

Santana
Santa Rita

São
João

São Martinho
Bareiros

Reid's
Hotel

see Funchal map

① **Funchal**

Jardim Botânico,
Jardim dos Loiros

Quinta da
Boa Vista

São Gonçalo

Santa Maria

Jardim Orquídeas

102

Madeira

pocket guide

Packed with all the information you need

What to See
Comprehensive coverage of Madeira's attractions:
lush scenery, historic towns, highlands and much more

What to Do
From colourful carnivals to invigorating walks: how to
make the most of your leisure time

Cultural Tips
Pirate raids and Madeira wine: giving you a deeper
understanding of the island's heritage

Practical Advice
Where to stay, dining out, and how to get around:
reliable recommendations and expert travel advice

www.insightguides.com/berlitz

£5.99

ISBN 978-178-004-132-2

00599

9 781780 041322